ENHANCING WRITING THROUGH IMAGERY

Using mental imagery to encourage confidence in creative expression

Karin K. Hess

Trillium Press
New York

Trillium Press, Inc.
PO Box 209
Monroe, New York 10950
(914) 783-2999

Printed in the United States of America
ISBN: 0-89824-152-9

A Letter

I used to see pictures in my head –
More than most, I think,
but then I was told that it was bad –

"Lazy girl, why do you sit and daydream so?"

"Idle hands a devil's workshop makes."
And (the teacher) stamped her foot and mocked.

"Why do you stare so with those big blue eyes?"
and the children singsonged,
"Big eyes, big eyes,"
and the pictures dimmed a little.

I resisted for a long, long time,
laughing at the grownups –
"You can't get at the pictures in my head,"
but child of conformity, my family,
and the church,
The pictures faded and lost their color.

I grew old, and life grew hard and always busy –

So many different hats to wear,
I ached for the solace of pictures in my head,

but they had fled.

But then one spring you came
to guide me through the tunnels of my mind,

and I caught a glimpse again
of a little girl, beneath a catalpa tree,
softly singing,
and smiling at the pictures in her head.

—*Catherine Reynolds*

Like most people who experience formal imagery training for the first time, Catherine Reynolds, a teacher, felt compelled to put into words what she'd known since she was a child – that the use of visualization and imagination is a healthy and natural act and cannot be ridiculed or repressed without denying a very important part of ourselves.

There is nothing mysterious or complicated about the activities in this book. They work because they begin with the writer and not the expectation of a finished product. They teach writers to reach within themselves, trust in whatever they find there and share their findings with others using written language.

ACKNOWLEDGMENTS

I wish to extend an affectionate thanks to teachers Julianna Repasky, Char Large and Dorothy Ramundo for their encouragement, creative ideas, and willingness to involve the students of North Warren Regional High School and Clarkstown South Sr. High School in many of the writing activities in this book.

A special thanks to Rita Baragona for the illustrations, to student Peter Packman for his rendition of the brain hemispheres and to Char Large and Cindy Schrick for manuscript preparation.

To mentors, Dr. Joe Khatena and Dr. Beverly-Colleene Galyean, for helping me to expand my understanding of imagery.

TABLE OF CONTENTS

CHAPTER

Imagery is...
imagination
thought
skill
emotion

Jennifer, grade four

CHAPTER ONE

An Overview

What is imagery?

Imagery is a process whereby a person can visualize an object, event or situation in his mind. These visual pictures represent photographic records of object, interactions and impressions of the external environment. They are often vivid, highly detailed representations of real-life experiences. While images may draw upon previous memories, specific experiences are not prerequisite to the process. The mind is capable of combining previous experiences in a way that produces "thoughts" which form the content of the images. These visualizations are most vivid when the mind is least distracted by interfering thoughts. As one focuses on a particular image, the mind automatically begins to slow down and limit the number of distractions and thought messages. The creative process (Imagination) becomes more active. This "stilling of the mind" increases the vividness and clarity of an image. The longer the mind remains in this restful, visual state, the longer the image will be projected in the mind's eye. The more a person uses his power to visualize, the greater control he will have over the skill. When you image, you become a projectionist capable of speeding up, slowing down or stilling a particular picture. The slowing down of the picture provides a detailed means to examine the elements in such a way that the individual gains new thoughts and emotional perspectives. (Bagley & Hess, 1984)

Is imagery like meditation?

Meditation, very simply, involves the following steps:
(1) getting into an erect but relaxed posture, keeping the spine straight
(2) becoming aware of the breath and beginning to breathe rhythmically
(3) voluntarily concentrating on either a visual or auditory focal point to achieve one-pointedness of mind and
(4) reaching a point of prolonged or perfect concentration, i.e.,meditation. The primary difference between imagery and meditation comes with the fourth step. Imagery puts the imager in control of a problem solving situation, looking for options, symbols, etc. in the images experienced. Meditation quite often begins with the same object of concentration and leads to the release of powerful forces stored in the unconscious in the form of revelations or realizations. (Satchidanada, 1975) After meditation, a feeling of calm remains. The same is true of imagery. Also present is sometimes a need to create or be productive. Because the body is relaxed and the mind is focused,

much more can be accomplished in a short amount of time. Both imagery and meditation are used in educational settings successfully because they address the need that all humans have to be both active and passive in an alternating rhythmical way. The activity planned after imagery grounds the energy collected during the imagery experience; thus writing becomes a natural release for creative energy. (Rozman, 1975)

What makes imagery unique?

Dr. Akhter Ahsen, known internationally for his work with eidetic imagery states that the basic unit of eidetic therapy is the ISM, a three-segment experience recorded in the form of a full-blown visual picture. The IMAGE (I) which portrays a situation, the SOMATIC (S) state which represents body feelings and emotions attached to the image and the MEANING (M) of that situation/image are all contained as a single unit, the visual image being the central focus, or bond of the ISM. During each significant emotional encounter, whatever is important in the conscious field of the person is spontaneously preserved in detail for later reference and stored in the brain. It can be played back long afterwards. These experiences continue to be recorded throughout our lives, yet the third component, meaning, is not readily cognitized before the age of five, explains Anna Dolan, Chief of Psychiatry at Yonkers General Hospital. These meanings may be generated later in life through the recall of specific ISM's that are causing imbalances that affect the individual's feeling states and self-concept.

Although the therapist uses this knowledge to explore the psyche, we as educators can use the ISM to unlock meanings in literature, build new layers of meaning for old concepts and create intended meanings by calling attention to images and the feelings that surround them. The vast storehouse of past encounters, or ISM's will become the basis for each writer's unique style. The writing itself serves as the vehicle through which the writer can clarify, modify and validate his own meanings.

Why must the individual communicate these meanings?

If we look at Joe Khatena's Multidimensional Interactive Creative Imagination Imagery Model (see Figure 1-1) we can see that the individual, represented by the large rectangle in the center, interacts with many and varied influences. Through his senses, he takes in information concerning the physical, social, cultural and universal ENVIRONMENT. It is then acted upon, stored and retrieved as needed, resulting in the desire to COMMUNICATE the EMERGENT IMAGES in a variety of ways (writing, art, music, discussion, etc.). It is the feedback from others that will MOTIVATE the individual to continue to be creative or make modifications in how these ideas are shared. The accompanying FEELINGS about the experience will directly effect any future encounters with his outside world.

The individual with positive feelings about generating and expressing a creative ideas and images will become more aware of his environment and open himself up to creative influences outside of himself, in the COSMOS.

Again, the implications are that we, as educators, can create new ENVIRONMENTS to be explored. With training, students can learn to build greater layers of MEANING and greater levels of AWARENESS with regard to the world around them. A supportive environment that encourages creative expression of original ideas will heighten MOTIVA-TION for future learning and reinforce positive FEELINGS about the self.

Multidimensional Interactive
Creative Imagination Imagery Model

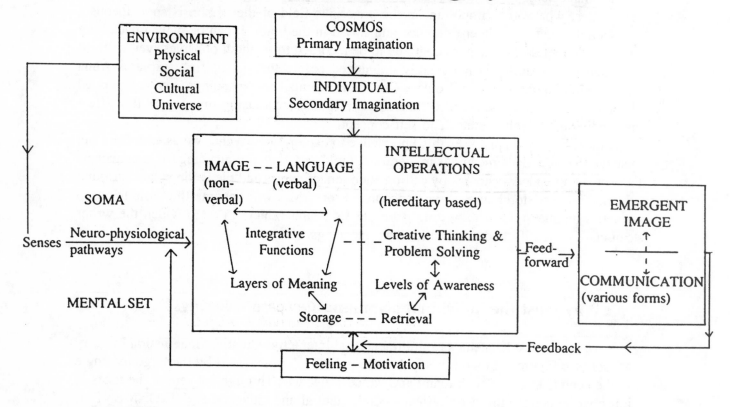

Figure 1-1
© Copyright 1983 by Joe Khatena. Reprinted with permission of the author.

4

"Creativity has not only made the human race unique in Nature: what is more important for the individual, it gives value and purpose to human existence. Creativity requires more than technical skills and logical thought; is also needs the cultivation and collaboration of the appositional (right) mind."

Joseph E. and Glenda M. Bogen, "The Other Side of the Brain III: The Corpus Callossum and Creativity"

CHAPTER TWO

The Imaging Mind and Body

Without getting too technical, I'd like to explain a little about how the brain works and what happens during imaging. You as the teacher, are sure to get questions from students and will feel more comfortable if you have basic facts "under your belt" before you begin. I also strongly suggest that you refer to the Bibliography of Suggested Readings after you've begun to use imagery to have a clearer understanding of it. Since imagery brings the mind and body together, both will be discussed.

What happens to the body during imagery?

Because of the similarities between imagery and meditation, I will share some research findings with regard to meditation. (Funderburk, 1977) Physiological changes occur during meditation. Much of this is due to the attention paid to bringing the mind and body into harmony using posture and breath and then sustaining that harmony. Research indicates that the following have been observed during meditation:

1. MUSCULAR ACTIVITY: Muscular activity is slight but the capacity for voluntary muscular action remains. (This lack of movement of the body during imagery or meditation increases the ability to concentrate because students do not need to "fidget," or move continually.)

2. BLOOD PRESSURE: Studies done with patients having high blood pressure showed that during and after meditation, blood pressure remained lowered. Even in patients who discontinued meditating, the blood pressure remained lowered for up to four weeks. (Using imagery on a regular basis could indeed regulate a more healthy blood pressure.)

3. HEART RATE: During meditation heart rate decreases by an average of 5-6 beats per minute. (You can prove this to your students by asking them to take their pulses before and after using imagery.)

4. RESPIRATION: There is a decrease in both amplitude and rate of respiration. (Make sure that students breathe through the nose, not the mouth. The brain sets on top of the nasal passage, thus the connection between breath and brain activity.)

5. BLOOD LACTATE LEVELS: High blood lactate levels associated with anxiety symptoms, decrease during meditation. (Guided fantasies that take a person to a pleasant and tranquil scene are often used in stress management programs for this very reason.)

For a more detailed look at each of the above studies, please refer to *Science Studies Yoga* (see Bibliography of Suggested Readings).

It won't take too many sessions before students begin to tell you that they are feeling relaxed and refreshed after an imagery exercise. Some students may ask to lie on the floor during imagery. I usually allow them the freedom to do what is most comfortable when first introducing imagery. Eventually, though, you will want to reinforce the idea that the spine should be straight, (not stiff) and sitting in comfortable cross-legged position is probably the most beneficial. If you have a student who tends to fall asleep, (this can happen) then you should suggest an erect sitting position.

Does relaxation enhance the imagery experience?

In order for there to be a progressive flow of the imagery process, four conditions must be met. (Bagley & Hess, 1984) They are:

1. The imager IDENTIFIES with a visual, audio or kinesthetic "picture" and immediately begins to draw upon previous meanings and/or various concepts, establishing a starting point for the imagery exercise.
2. The mind and body are RELAXED in order to allow for an uninterrupted flow of images to appear. Often special music, autosuggestion or a tranquil scene to be imaged are used to achieve this relaxation.
3. The imager ACCEPTS the images that appear without feeling the need to analyze, verbalize or judge them. The imager may wish to use his imagination to change or "play with" images and ideas.
4. Meanings are generated once CONCENTRATION has been achieved. Usually both intellectual and emotional insights are revealed through the images that are evoked. To heighten concentration, encourage students to pay close attention to details by suggesting that they focus on such aspects as color, texture, shape, etc.

Without these conditions being met images will remain superficial, only vague expressions of what the imager thinks he should see. You should expect this to happen when you first introduce imagery to your students. With practice however the highest level of association, that of interaction with images, will occur. (Ahsen, 1977) To encourage this, you may wish to use a relaxation exercise with students who need "extra" calming down before you begin the imagery. I've included two relaxation exercises that you may wish to use with your students. The first was written by a teacher, Barbara Saltzman and the second by a student, Meridith Glickman. (Both follow the guidelines for writing a guided fantasy.)

7

Fur
by Barbara Saltzman

Sit back and find a comfortable position
Close your eyes
Breathe in deeply
Exhale slowly
Do it again
Visualize a large piece of fur on the ground
Go and lie down on your back on the fur
Feel the fur caress you as you sink into it
Feel the warmth against your back
Feel the softness and silkiness of the hairs with your hands
Wrap the fur around you
Luxuriate in the warmth and security of your fur cocoon
Stay there until the count of ten and then open your eyes

Forest
by Meridith Glickman (Gr. 10)

Relax and sit in a comfortable position
Inhale...exhale...
Picture yourself lying in a bed of thick moss and leaves
Feel the slight warmth of the escaping sun that the tall redwood trees are letting through
Smell the aroma of dew-covered leaves...and pines
Hear the melodious concertos sung by many kinds of tropical birds
As the band of birds flies by, see the exotic patterns made by the beautiful feathers
Hear the crackling water of a nearby waterfall
Walk to the spring through the thick moss
Feel the cool water glide through your fingers
See the sun just beginning to set in the distance
See the beautiful rainbow of colors
Feel the slight chill that has come upon the forest
When I count to ten you will be back n the classroom.

What happens to the mind during imagery?

In the past twenty years, brain research has become more intense, uncovering many fascinating facts and theories. One of the most interesting findings is that of the dual nature of the brain. Each hemisphere is capable of operating independently of the other and of processing the same information in a different way (Rico, 1983). The left and right hemispheres are connected by the corpus callosum, a band of 200 million nerve fibers.

If you could look down into someone's head as in Figure 2-1, you might see that the left hemisphere processes only one stimulus at a time in an orderly and sequential way, while on the right, a cluster of stimuli are simultaneously being processed. The left produces logical, linear thinking and relies heavily upon previously accumulated organized information. The right hemisphere has a greater capacity for dealing with complex information for which no learned program is available, or intuitive thinking. Both types of thinking are important and necessary in learning, yet all too often, only the logical side is exercised once children enter school.

Regardless of the hemisphere, all information is automatically transformed and stored in the brain as an image or symbol (Samuels & Samuels, 1975). Each of the brain's 100-200 billion neurons is capable of storing up to 5 billion bits of information. Thinking takes place only when a connection is made (at the synapse) between these stored bits of information (Galyean, 1980). Because imagery encourages freedom of thought in the form of visual, audio and kinesthetic images, it stimulates the kind of thinking that takes place in the right hemisphere of the brain and increases integration of the right and left once the written interpretation of images begins.

How can I explain the brain's functions to my students?

An easy way to illustrate to students how the brain looks and acts is to ask them to make two fists and place them together with fingernails touching (Clark, 1983) (see Figure 2-2). The arms become the spinal cord, bringing information from the senses to the brain to be processed. The fingernails represent the corpus callosum which connects the hemispheres. Pinky fingers are the occipital lobe, or vision center; the middle fingers are the parietal lobe or motor area; thumbs represent the frontal lobe where higher thinking functions take place.

Now separate the hands and look only at one of the hemispheres. The arm-wrist area, often called the reptilian brain, represents the simplest and oldest brain system. Here we find the seat of such automatic functions as circulation and respiration. If you think of the functions common to the first reptiles on earth, then you can identify what takes place in the reptilian or lower brain.

Next look at the area of the palm. This is called the old mammalian brain or limbic system. Just as the first mammals experienced emotions of anxiety, rage, pleasure and grief, unknown to reptilian society, our emotions are based here, in the midbrain. The limbic system is made up of 5 glands and is responsible for our emotional expressions and interactions that enhance or inhibit memory. What occurs in the limbic system directly effects attention, retention and motivation (Galyean, 1980). It is the hypothalamus gland that secretes a series of hormones, endorphins, which in turn anesthetize the action of the other glands when a situation is perceived as painful or unpleasant. The result is that information does not reach the neocortex to be processed. The converse is also true. A learning situation that is pleasant will be processed and retained more readily.

The curled fingers, representing about 5/6 of the total brain are the higher or new mammalian brain. Here sensory data is processed, decisions are made and action is initiated. The language area (temporal lobe), is located just below the middle knuckle on the left hand (hemisphere) and the thumbs can be seen as the prefrontal and frontal lobes. The prefrontal area which develops before the frontal lobe, is the center for abstract thinking, logical processing and being able to create. The frontal (or forehead) area is the last to evolve and responsible for the need for global unity, higher forms of love, empathy, ESP, friendship and beauty. Without these a person may develop intellect and use it destructively. It could make the difference between an Adolf Hitler or an Albert Schweitzer personality.

> **Because imagery involves interaction between the imager and the images, it helps to develop the deeply personal skills of introspection, bonding, unity, trust and empathy.** (Galyean, 1983)

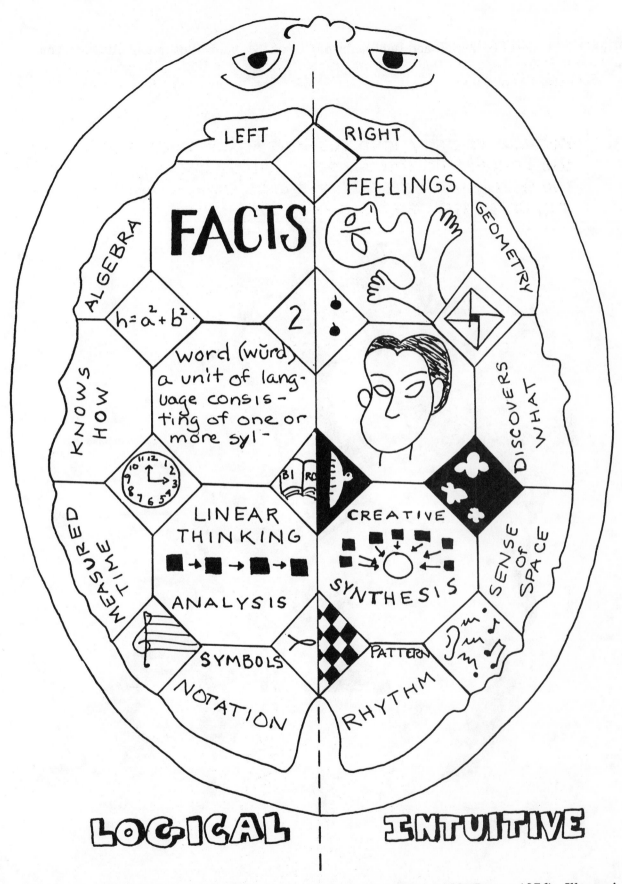

Figure 2-1: The left and right hemispheres of the brain, (Rico,1983)(Buzan,1976). Illustration, Rita Baragona.

Figure 2-2: A model of the left and right hemispheres of the brain. Illustration, Peter Packman.

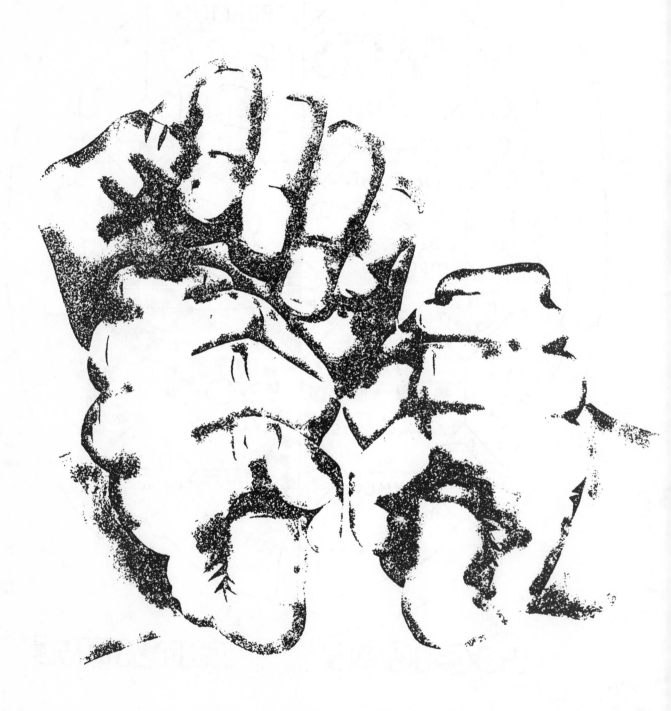

"We. . .write to heighten our own awareness of life. . .to expand our world, when we feel strangled, constricted, lonely . . .When I don't write I feel my world shrinking. I feel I lose my fire, my color."

Anaïs Nin (*The Diary of Anaïs Nin*)

CHAPTER THREE

Imagery in the Classroom

Why should imagery be used in education?

Research indicates that intelligence is directly related to multi-sensory processing (Galyean, 1980) and maximum retention over long term is greatly enhanced when all lobes of the brain are simultaneously stimulated. This occurs most often during a daydream or alpha state (see Figure 3-1). This is a time when the brain is relaxed but alert, calm but in control of higher level thinking functions.

Most of our waking hours are spent in beta, a wide awake, ready-for-action state of mind. Our bodies are usually moving or at least tense and erect. The brain waves during beta are like that of a motor boat and we, the drivers, must be ready for anything in our paths. As we close our eyes and begin to regulate breathing, the mind slows down and although we are still alert, we are traveling at a slower speed and can take in more scenery. In an alpha state we are able to quiet "mind chatter" and better concentrate on an idea. We can also "tune out" noises and distractions around us.

As both the body and mind become more relaxed, theta waves are emitted from the brain. We slip closer to sleep or delta. When students understand the different levels of brain activity they feel more in control of their minds during imagery and know that they are not being hypnotized or put to sleep!

Imagery has been found to be the single most effective curriculum intervention strategy for simultaneously stimulating the four lobes of the brain because it involves mental stimulation of all of the senses and the kinesthetic body, higher level thinking skills, cognitive information to be processed, and a chance to respond emotionally as well as intellectually.

IMAGERY ADDRESSES THE NEEDS OF THE WHOLE PERSON.

It is also interesting to note that during periods of extreme stress, the neocortex, which is responsible for higher level thinking, begins to shut down and only rote learning can take place under these conditions.

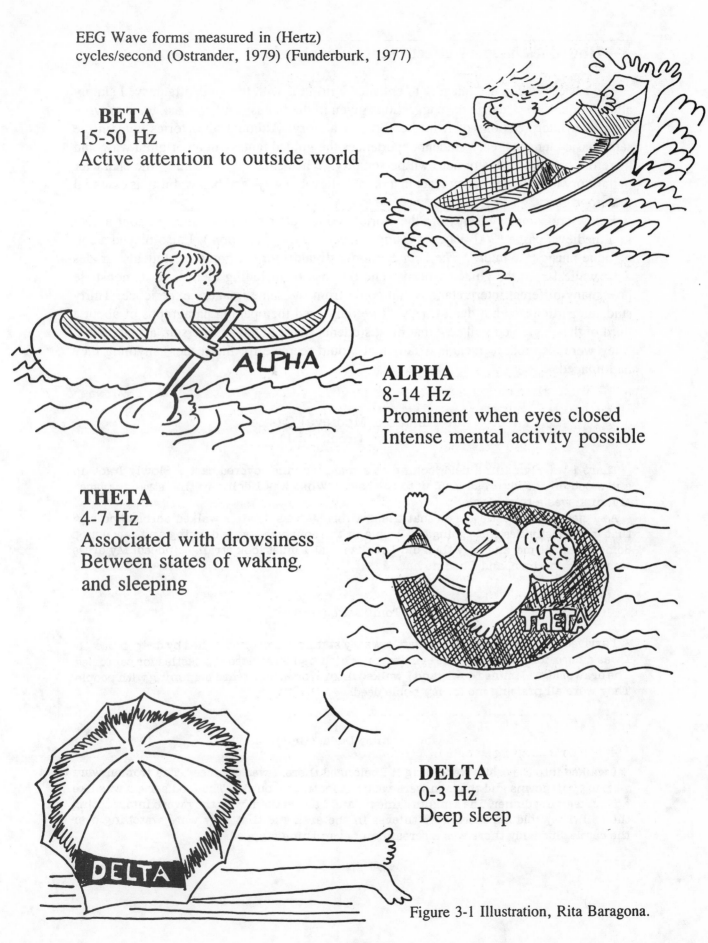

EEG Wave forms measured in (Hertz)
cycles/second (Ostrander, 1979) (Funderburk, 1977)

BETA
15-50 Hz
Active attention to outside world

ALPHA
8-14 Hz
Prominent when eyes closed
Intense mental activity possible

THETA
4-7 Hz
Associated with drowsiness
Between states of waking,
and sleeping

DELTA
0-3 Hz
Deep sleep

Figure 3-1 Illustration, Rita Baragona.

15

How does imagery effect creative expression?

The easiest way to use imagery to enhance writing is with the guided fantasy. I simply allow students to visualize the suggestions given in the fantasy and later ask them to write their own interpretations of it in the form of a story. Although the stories contain the same basic elements, each student experiences the guided fantasy in an original way, and therefore brings to it his or her own personality. When students "become" the character in the story to be written, they react in a more believable way, and believability is essential to a good story.

Below are samples taken from the stories written after a guided fantasy about a visit to a medieval castle (*200 Ways of Using Imagery in the Classroom*). I also played a soft baroque music ("Winter," *The Four Seasons*, Vivaldi) for the group of students, grades 7-12 while I read the guided fantasy. The purpose of including them is to demonstrate how many different interpretations can come from the same imagery experience. Thirty students participated but due to space, I've only used the opening paragraphs of about a third of the class. You will note that most students wrote in the first person, as instructed. They were also told to include details that would recreate for the reader, anything they had imaged.

A Visit to a Medieval Castle
by Patricia Tironi, (Gr.11)

There I was, lying in a field looking at a massive, vine-covered castle. Slowly I got up and stood on the dirt road leading to the castle. What was I doing in this strange place? My mind was a total blank.

As I neared the castle, I saw that the drawbridge was down. I walked across and saw that many festivities were going on. People in the courtyard were dancing and carousing. Some stared at me, and only then did I realize that I must look strange, indeed! My dress was filthy and torn, and I had no hat.

by Tom Klein, (Gr.9)

I arrived at the rustic castle in a battle-weary state, my armor scorched by dragon breath. I was a hero, for I had killed the evil dragon which had terrorized the castles for centuries. The drawbridge slammed down, and I walked into an open courtyard brimming with people. They were all praising me for my noble deed.

by Jennifer Duda, (Gr.8)

I walked into the castle wondering if I belonged there. I was confused. The women were wearing ball gowns and the men were wearing footmen's outfits. The food served was like a Thanksgiving dinner. The knights came in, and I asked them why they were interrupting the ball. They told me there were thieves in the area and that they were watching over the castle. Suddenly there was a scream and everything stopped.

by Laura A Gebhart, (Gr.11)

As we approached the massive drawbridge that led to the beautiful stone castle, the horses that towed our sparkling white carriage whinnied. A lot of people were in the courtyard, talking, laughing, and dancing to the music played by an orchestra. It was a sunny day and the birds and butterflies seemed to be as joyful as I was.

Once inside the castle, I was escorted to the ornately decorated banquet hall. My soft white dress flowed smoothly as I walked. A wonderful aroma was in the air and all kinds of delightful food was on the table. Turkey with stuffing, mashed potatoes, cranberries, fresh vegetables, prime rib, wine, and every dessert imaginable was available in abundance.

by Mike Rosania, (Gr.9)

I woke up looking at a dark eerie castle. I was dressed like Robin Hood would have been. Inside the castle wall were poor-looking peasants, cooking their meal over a fire in front of their hut. Beyond the rows of huts stood the large marble castle with a grand hallway which I took to the ballroom. Inside the huge room was banquet with many people, some dancing, some eating.

by Susan Gwinnett, (Gr.10)

As the tall stone drawbridge is slowly lowered, I hear a lot of noise coming from inside. I enter the gigantic castle. Hundreds of people swarm around me and are bowing. I feel a sense of greatness and a sudden rush of power. As I walk into the bright, colorful dining hall, I see a long table covered with food wine. I sit in a huge, gold-covered chair and allow people to feed me.

by Kim Miller, (Gr.10)

As I enter the garden, a soft breeze ruffles my hair slightly, and billows my chiffon skirt. The gardener has obviously been at work here - everything is perfect. Darkness is quickly approaching, and the cool dampness of evening air is now evident in the autumn breeze. I return to the courtyard where several maids are tidying up. I proceed through the wide arch, to the main hall in the castle. The walls are cold, hard, marble, as are the floors, inlaid with ornate designs, the largest of which was under my feet—the family crest.

by Tom Gilmore, (Gr.11)

As I stand in front of the gray stone castle surrounded by a moat filled with frogs and water lilies, the heavy wooden drawbridge begins to open. With many creaks and groans, finally one great thud sends dust from the powdery dirt road as the heavy old door opens. I am greeted by many a lord and lady, dressed in splendid costumes, anxiously awaiting my visit. Why? I am a prince from a far off land. They escort me to the great ballroom where a feast has been prepared in my honor.

by Wendy Unangst, (Gr.11)

I stood there in the stormy darkness with the wind whipping at my hair. I wasn't sure why I was back here—I had promised myself never to come back. As I watched, the drawbridge opened, and the guard at the gate greeted me. I walked to the courtyard remembering the fountain and smiling fondly at the laughing children. I was home at last!

by Kathleen Brennan, (Gr.11)

"I'm lost. I knew I should have stayed with my company. Of all the people it has to be me who gets lost in the jungles of Viet Nam," Lance said out loud as he wandered. He had been warned several times not to go off the path to look at the fascinating vegetation, but he didn't listen; now he was lost.

Although some students opted to write in the present tense while others chose the past, there is evidence of several commonalities in these and other writing samples done after a guided fantasy activity. Time and time again I have observed that:
1. Details and descriptions are vivid.
2. Hints of characters' moods and emotions are present.
3. Choice of words is more evocative than informative, thus creating a clear mental picture in the reader's mind's eye.
4. Stories contain events and scenes that are believable even when imaginary.
5. Individual interpretations are as unique as the writers creating them.

IMAGERY ENHANCES ORIGINALITY

What Do Students Say about Imagery?

Each time I introduce imagery to the people taking my graduate courses at least one high school teacher questions whether the students will actually close their eyes and take it seriously. I expect this reaction and try to assure teachers that it will work if *they* believe that it will. I even share some comments from students that I've worked with and suggest that they try it at least once before class meets again. The skeptics usually shake their heads, whisper something to a colleague and agree to try it, (only because it's part of the assignment!) I always look forward to the next class because without fail, teachers return, excited about imagery and writing. They find what I've found time and time again—kids love using imagery!

Below are comments from students (grades 8-12) who attended four sessions of creative writing with me. They are taken from the written seminar evaluation forms completed by each student. You will notice that their comments focus not only on writing, but most importantly on a "good feeling" about themselves. REMEMBER—most students can't write because they *think* that they can't write. Imagery validates all of the past learning experiences that they've had, allowing them to "call back" and build upon them to gain new insights. Imagery gives them a reason to continue to learn and expand this wonderful storehouse that we call the mind.

Michelle: "The seminars were fascinating and opened up a whole new perspective for my poetry and creative writing. Thank you!"

Sue: "It really helped me understand the technique of writing. I really think I leaned a lot. I know I like it. But most and best of all, I learned how to relax myself."

Tom: "I gained a new tool to make ideas for creative writing. I think it will be a valuable help in the future."

Elaine: "I learned to build images in my mind, and to express these images better. Do it again!"

Jennifer: "I thought that creating our workshops and doing the other exercises to get ideas for writing helped me a lot. I enjoyed the seminars very much and I felt I learned more than I expected."

Adam: "It was very interesting. It showed me just how deep your mind is. The images really made me relax. Thank you for opening my mind. You helped me relax to think up ideas."

Laura: "I learned that I have a *great* imagination! It was fun to let it fun wild. I learned that you can create a very vivid image to the reader just by using the right words to describe what's in your mind's eye. This was very unique and relaxing. It helped me a lot to be able to put my feelings or what I saw into words. It was a very enlightening experience."

Patti: "I learned that any time, I could image to obtain ideas and thoughts to help me write better. I created a workshop in my mind that I can go to at anytime to get ideas. The imaging really works, and I'm glad I learned something about it!"

Alyssa: "I am now able to produce many images in my mind where before I just tried to 'think up' ideas without really seeing them. When I closed my eyes, I really relaxed and could form images very easily in my mind."

Tom: "I think I learned more about getting ideas for writing in this seminar than I learned anywhere else. Imagery helped me get details of things."

Wendy: "Imagery is a valuable tool to use in writing, plus a healing process in your whole life. It was one of the best experiences in my entire life."

Kathy: "This seminar helped me with my writing skills, and the development of my creativity. It also helped me to gain a better understanding of myself."

Mike: "I found a part of myself that I never knew I had."

Jenny: "I learned that through relaxation I could image and let my mind 'flow'. It was *fantastic*; as if I have discovered a new part of my brain that has been dormant for too long—an exciting new realm of thought. If this isn't a valid learning experience, I don't know what is! Thanks!"

And what about the long range effects? Do students continue to use imagery? Some do. Donna, a former seventh grade student of mine, sent a letter to me more than a year after I left that school. In it she wrote: "I know a lot of people are still imaging but they need a person to tell them what to think about, like you did. So at parties I usually get that part."

Imagery does make a lasting impression when students take it seriously. It is important to teach the imaging skills found in the Introductory Imagery Activities sections so that students can use imagery independently with confidence and success.

What kind of results can I expect?

It would be difficult to make blanket statements about the success of using imagery if I had not experimented with it for many years with people of all ages and ability levels. I have used imagery with preschool children through senior citizens. I have worked with the gifted as well as the learning disabled. I have used imagery to teach math, science, social studies, reading and language. I have used imagery to develop skills in sports, dance, drama, writing and art. Some students accept imagery immediately and others take some winning over before they admit that it's something that can increase their abilities. The bottom line is, that it works. It works with all ages, all abilities, all skills. Of course, the degrees of success depend upon the individuals, but I have never seen it not work.

With writing, the results are measurable because you have something to compare. You can save writing before using imagery and after using imagery. As a matter of fact, I encourage you to do just that. Have students write about a topic, introducing it in your usually way, using any writing program that you now use. Then have the students image the topic in the form of a guided fantasy and ask them to write. They, as well as you, will be surprised at the ideas that imagery generates. Below is a sample of just that. When the movie "E.T," came out, I suggested to a group of sixth grade students, who had never used imagery before, that they write a paragraph about having a flying bicycle. When they finished, I lead them through a guided fantasy from *200 Ways of Using Imagery in the Classroom* about riding a flying bicycle and asked them to write again. Here is what Jeff Burdge wrote:

BEFORE: If I had a flying bike I would fly around the country and see all of the sites. Then when I got back I would go and tell my friends, and if they didn't believe me I'd show them how.

AFTER: My ride on the bike was fascinating. I saw my friends pedalling up a big hill. I say my house and all of my friends' houses. I saw Mt. Rushmore and the Rocky Mountains. It was beautiful. I have never done anything like it before in my life.

There was no geography lesson between the writings. There was no vocabulary development or English lesson of any kind either. The entire session only took about twenty minutes in all, yet something very definitely took place. The imagery unlocked the *real* experience of the flying bike! What you cannot see without looking at Jeff's actual paper is that even the handwriting shows a marked difference. The first paragraph shows that the pen was pressed harder onto the paper, leaving darker and larger letters. The words in the second paragraph are lighter, smaller and neater, reflecting, I think, a more relaxed and more confident hand.

IMAGERY UNLOCKS THE INNER WRITER BY MAKING THE SUBJECT BECOME A REAL EXPERIENCE.

"Man sees only what he's prepared to see."

Ralph Waldo Emerson

CHAPTER FOUR

Introductory Imagery Activities

Building the all-important foundation

Attempting to teach through imagery without preparation and understanding of the imagery process, can sometimes be worse than not using imagery at all. So often, teachers tell me that they have tried imagery or guided fantasy or relaxation with their classes but it didn't work out. The class didn't take it seriously. Parents and administrators asked questions that they could not answer. They were not sure enough of what they were doing to spend "valuable class time" on something that appeared to be a frill. The older the students, the more the concerns that were raised by teachers. High school students are old enough to know why they are learning in a certain way. For that matter, I believe that any student who asks about the imagery process, deserves to be given as honest and intellectual an answer as you can give. For that reason it is essential that you and your students understand what it is you are going to be doing with your minds. Knowledge really is power.

The eleven activities in this section are provided as an introductory course in what mental imagery is. Spending some class time during a two to three week period with these exercises will build a solid foundation for future imagery learning experiences. Students can ease into this "new way" of thinking about themselves and their intellectual growth and can take the time to examine each aspect of the imagery process, (such as vividness, memory, imagination, etc.) to understand better its importance to the larger picture—enhancing learning through imagery.

The Introductory Imagery Activities are progressive and should be followed in the suggested order, 1-11, although there are optional activities included with the eleven. CONTROLLABILITY, activity #8, offers an in depth exploration of how to summon and control images. You may wish to use only parts of it or omit it altogether, since activity #7, CHANGING AND CONTROLLING IMAGES, also covers this component. AFTER-IMAGES, another optional activity (#10), provides a basis for contrasting mental imagery to images that are seen without physically being there. Whether you choose to use the optional activities or not, is not as important as simply reading them over to gain a better understanding for yourself. You may wish to use the Introductory Writing Activities in conjunction with this section or as a follow up to it. Included with PICTURES FROM THE PAST, PLEASANT EXPERIENCES, MULTI-SENSORY IMAGES, GUIDED FANTASY, CONTROLLABILITY, and VIVIDNESS are suggested writing activities also.

Below is an overview of the Introductory Imagery Activities and the skills that are introduced:

Each activity provides a classroom dialogue to give you a general sense of how the lesson could progress. This is only a guide and you should feel free to adapt it to your individual style and needs, realizing that with imagery you cannot easily predict which direction the discussion, or processing out, will take. Since you are tapping the uniqueness in all students, the "typical" response to a given question is now a thing of the past. General types of responses with brief explanations are given in the parentheses, ( ), after most discussion questions. Again, these only serve as a guide. Above all else, students *must* feel that whatever they share with the group is valid and acceptable. You do not have to agree with what is said. You do not have to believe what is said. But you must accept it without judgement and insist that everyone in the class does the same. A simple "thank you for sharing that," or "that's interesting" is enough. Don't try to analyze ideas or look for symbolism in the images. As a teacher, your primary role is that of one who shows students how to unlock their ideas and turn them into some form of creative expression. Should you become interested in interpreting symbols, wait until you complete the Introductory Imagery Activities and go on to MYTHS. Here you can discuss symbols without allowing it to become personalized. Two excellent references for symbolism are *A Dictionary of Symbols* Cirlot, J.E. (Philosophical Library, N.Y. 1976) and *Images and Symbols* Elaide, Mircea (Sheed & Ward, N.Y. 1969).

All imagery activities are set apart on the page by special type. This serves as a reminder to soften your voice tone, allow sufficient pausing at each set of . . . . (5 seconds to 2 minutes), dim the room lights if possible, and expect a wonderfully relaxed and creative experience. You may wish to position yourself so that you can see a clock with a second hand. This will help you to be aware of your pausing. You will feel that you are going very slowly, but remember, your mind is still in beta while the class has begun to slow down to alpha! Students are always telling me that they didn't have enough time to complete their imaging. *You can never go too slowly.*

It is suggested that students close their eyes. This helps to shut out visual stimuli in the room just as fine tuning gets rid of static. It also speeds up the process of moving to an alpha state of mind. There will always be some students who feel uncomfortable closing their eyes at first. Don't force the issue. Just suggest that they look down at their feet, laps or desks. Most students prefer to put their heads down on their desks or to stretch out on a carpeted floor. I have found that high school students relax much more quickly if you can get them on the floor.

Initially any body position is acceptable as long as the legs are uncrossed for longer exercises and no one is leaning on an arm or elbow. Eventually I suggest that the spine should be straight to allow for energy to flow through the body. This can be achieved in either a sitting or lying down position. If sitting, the legs may be crossed Indian-style or in the yoga lotus position. Students should be encouraged to experiment with different positions until they find one that suits them.

Once again, let me emphasize the importance of introducing imagery in a nonthreatening but serious manner. If you treat it as a frill, the students will never accept it as a valid learning experience. If you treat it as a scientifically proven way of tapping into creative potential, the doors you unlock will be infinite! Prepare them well for the journey.

WHAT DO YOU SEE?

Purpose

To demonstrate to the students how easy it is for the mind to create a whole from parts.

Materials

Overhead transparencies, "What do you see?" (APPENDIX)
Student page, "What do you see?" (APPENDIX)

Procedures

I would like to show you something. Look at it for a minute and then tell me what you see. (Project transparency #1. Allow for spontaneous guessing and discussion among students, while they look. Then ask,) How many people just saw dots and nothing else? What did anyone else see? (Accept all answers as correct. Some students will want to know what the "right" answer is...all answers are correct if that is what was seen.)

This time I want you to do the same thing, but please don't talk while you're looking. (Project transparency #2. Wait about one minute, then ask what was seen. Remember to accept all answers.)

In ancient times, people looked up into the sky and saw pictures in the stars. We call these pictures constellations and can recognize them by the picture they are supposed to represent. (Distribute student page.) I'd like you to look at these "dots" and see if you can create a constellation with them. Study each picture for a while until a central theme seems to emerge. Then draw the constellation. (Since these are real constellations, you may wish to have students turn papers in a different direction, upside-down, etc., to avoid this being a left brain recall drill of constellations. After drawing, ask if anyone would like to share what they saw. Accept the fact that there will be different answers as well as some who could not create 4 pictures. I would never suggest that you tell the class the actual names of the constellations; I don't even like including that information, but I know some will want to know. They are (A) Orion (B) Canis Major (C) Pegasus and (D) Scorpius.)

Processing Out

What side of the brain naturally puts parts together to make wholes? (Right) If a person can see a picture that hasn't been drawn yet, is that imagery? What can you say about the person who can only see the dots? (Left brain strongly dominant. Too much logic being used—thus blocking the image-making process.) Is there something wrong with a person if they cannot see a picture in the dots? (Be very careful not to let this idea get started. If you do have some students who had difficulty with this exercise, they will need to feel that it is OK, otherwise their progress will be hindered.)

Teacher Notes

It is important that the students can see a shape before it is drawn. This strengthens the ''seeing with the mind's eye'' concept. You may wish to point out to students that writing follows much the same process: words and fragments of ideas, when allowed to ''simmer'' will naturally form a central theme, which in turn can be expanded upon to give it greater clarity.

PICTURES FROM THE PAST

Purpose

To allow students to experience the most common form of visualization, the MEMORY IMAGE. The first activities explore the short-term memory and the next deal with long-term memory as it relates to the image-making process.

Materials

ACTIVITIES #1, #2, and #4 none. ACTIVITY #3, Student page, "Pictures from the Past" (APPENDIX)

ACTIVITY #1

Procedure

I'd like you to write down on a piece of paper, all that you ate for dinner last night. (Allow several minutes for everyone to finish. If for some reason, a student did not eat dinner, have him list food eaten at the most recent meal.)

Processing Out

In writing these items down, did anyone get a mental picture of any of the food? How about taste, smell or texture? (Sensory images are common.) Did anyone get a mental picture of anything else, like where you ate or who was with you? (Details are slowly being added to the image.) Did anyone have trouble remembering what they ate for dinner? (It is common to forget things that lack any emotional bond. Things that remain in the memory are those that involve a feeling or personal attachment.)

ACTIVITY #2

Procedure

(Position yourself where all can see you.) I'd like you to look at me for a minute, quietly. Notice what I'm wearing, colors, patterns and style. Observe the color of my hair, the shape of my face, eyes and mouth. Now I'd like you to close your eyes and see me in your mind's eye just as I look now. See my hair. . .face. . .eyes. . .what I'm wearing. . . . . . . .open your eyes and look once again. . . . . . . .now close your eyes and see me more clearly than the first time. (Pause for 15 seconds.) Open your eyes. (This activity may also be done with pairs of students, teacher narrating.)

Processing out

Would anyone like to share what they did or did not see? (Wait for responses. Accept all answers.) Were some things easier than others to see? (Clothing is usually easier than a face to image. Some may have seen parts but not the whole person. Some may have seen the room in the background or the teacher doing something "typical" for her/him to do. Accept all answers.) Did anyone see me more clearly the second time?

ACTIVITY #3

Procedure

(Distribute copies of the Student Page, "Pictures from the past".) I would like you to take a couple of minutes to try to describe things that you remember as a young child. Look at the list on the left side of the page. After reading each to yourself, write a brief description in the box to the right. If you do not have a memory to describe, skip it and go on to the next. You will not have to read these aloud. Pay attention to the ones that are the easiest to remember and write about. If you wish to go back and add to any of them, you may do so. (Allow 15 minutes so that there is time to reread and/or add to what has been written.)

Processing Out

Go down your list and put an 'X' after any memory that created a picture of any kind. (Pause.) Would anyone like to share what he or she saw or what evoked that image? For those who did see something, was it instantly vivid or did it gradually become clear? (Details will often create a clearer picture when they are added.) Of the ones you were able to describe, how many seemed to have an emotion tied to it? (The strongest emotions will usually be tied to the most clear memories. This is true of both positive and negative emotions.) Have you ever gotten a similar feeling when looking at old family photos? When hearing the name of a place you had visited in the past? When hearing a voice on the phone that you haven't heard for a long time? What can you say about feelings and memory images?

Teacher Notes

Some students may say that they did not "see" anything but have a definite sense of it and know what it looks like. They are using their intuitive sense and emotions, both evidence of Right Brain activity. It is important that they feel comfortable continuing in this way. That is their "mind's eye." Some may also mention that they became more relaxed as the activity continued, and that more images formed as they continued to write.

ACTIVITY #4

Procedure

For this activity we are going to focus on only one memory from your childhood, looking at all of the details of that time. You may experience some emotions, which, as we have learned, often accompany a memory image. If by chance, there are negative feelings that you do not wish to encourage, just open your eyes and wait for the rest to finish.

Sit comfortably and relax. Close your eyes and listen to your breathing become steady. Inhale to a silent count of 4 and exhale to a silent count of 4...(Wait for at least three of these counts before continuing.) See yourself going back in time to the first classroom that you remember...notice the desks...the walls...and blackboards...the floors...ceilings...and lights...find a window...and look outside...see your teacher at the teacher's desk...observe how the teacher is dressed...and the hair color...listen to the teacher speaking...now look at how you are dressed...and your friends...sit at your desk and scan the entire room slowly...find something in the classroom that brought you great joy when you went to school there...enjoy it again...(Pause for a full minute.) Scan the room one last time before you return to this classroom...as I count to 10, become more aware of your presence in this room...1...2...3...4...5...6...7...8...9...10...open your eyes.

Processing Out

How vivid were your images? Did they become more vivid as details were recalled? What feelings did you experience? Did you feel as if you were actually "in" the room or just looking into a picture of the room? (Most will feel as if they were there.) Could you hear the teacher's voice? other noises and voices? Did you experience anything not suggested to you? (Some jump from one classroom to another. Some can only focus on one part of the classroom and not others. Some students will say that the walls seemed dull rather than bright as they "thought" they would remember them. The explanation is probably rooted in reality and their perception of reality. The use of imagery in therapy is used for this reason; the mind's recorded image is more accurate than conscious recall.) Can you make a comparison between long and short-term memory?

Teacher Notes

If you feel that more experience is needed with memory images, you may wish to have students image some of the following:
    a favorite childhood story or book being read to them
    a birthday party
    a special vacation or trip
    a best friend, (real or imaginary)
    a favorite pet (possibly emotional subject, but a valuable experience as a writing stimulus)
    a childhood room and special toy

Writing Activity

Find a family photo that has special meaning for you. Study the picture and then close your eyes and relive the time from which it is taken. When you feel a central theme emerging, begin to write...IN THE FIRST PERSON AND PRESENT TENSE. (You may want to ask students to bring in the pictures and do the activity in class.) (You may wish to do this activity later on in the term, again, to compare the writing/imaging progress.)

Here is a wonderful example of how a picture of a rose arbor cut from a magazine, sparked memories from the childhood of art teacher, John W. Hobart III. He said at the time he was writing it that the ideas "flowed" onto the page very easily. You will notice that he begins by remembering first as a boy, then as a teenager and young man and finally as an adult. It is the rose arbor that has tied the series of memories together and brought the story full circle.

Time to Smell the Roses
John W. Hobart III

I remember, long ago, spending my summer vacations and weekends at my grandparents' home, working in their yard. My father would pick me up each Friday night during the school year and return me to my mother's house thirty miles away, on Sunday nights. The time would reverse on summer vacations. My parents were separated when I was young, and we continued this court-ordered arrangement for many years through my adolescence.

My grandparents' home was unassuming in appearance—just a two-story frame house built around nineteen hundred, when the Ontario and Western Railway was in its heyday. My grandfather retired from the railroad as an electrical engineer many years earlier. I was the caretaker of their yard, which to me then, seemed a large spread, though now, I realize, was only two city lots in size. My fondest memories of those well-loved people during that time are of them helping me clean their yard, and especially of a grand old arbor which ran the full length of their home. The security transmitted through their love, constant encouragement, and pride in me, has lasted me throughout the years. The arbor was the showpiece of their yard. When they would tire, my grandfather, who many years before, had purchased one of those four person free-standing swings, would say to my grandmother, "come on Sally, time to swing," and I would continue to work at cutting the grass or weeding the well- manicured area beneath the rose arbor. The fragrance of our roses was transmitted throughout the neighborhood, and many people would stop by while walking on the street and say, "that's some nice smelling roses you've got there, son." I used to beam.

The years passed by and Dad no longer came to pick me up on weekends, for I had a job. I wanted to make my grandparents proud of me. It took some time, but eventually I made enough money to buy a car, and I wanted to do something nice for those two old people I loved so dearly. I had their old earthen driveway blacktopped near the arbor. It looked just great. Several more years passed and I took my best girl to their home to show her off to them, and them to her. I began noticing each time I visited that the house and grounds became more and more in a state of disrepair. No longer did they have the strength to do those things we did together beneath the arbor. Several years went by after I was married, and grandmother passed away, then grandfather. The house and grounds were sold for a meager sum to settle the estate.

It bothers me to ride past the place, now, although several times a year I'll park my car a block away and walk to the front of that yard and look at the roses which still climb over that grand old arbor. On the last visit I saw a little boy kneeling at the base of one of the columns clipping briars from a vine and I couldn't help remarking, "that's some nice smelling roses you've got there, son."

IMAGINATION IMAGERY

Purpose

To introduce students to the second most common form of imagery, the IMAGINATION IMAGE.

MATERIALS

None.

Procedure

Dreams and daydreams are examples of IMAGINATION IMAGES. They may have some bits of information in them from your memory or your real life, but they also contain things that could not happen in the real world. IMAGINATION IMAGES are sometimes used in problem solving. A person can mentally "play" with solutions and use some of the ideas gained to solve the problem practically. It's simply a case of taming a wild idea. Innovations in special effects for movies, new T.V. commercials, story lines, theater set designs, musical compositions, and art work and (even) inventions can get their beginning during an imagination image. Using the left side of the brain to analyze and evaluate solutions will greatly diminish your creativity. As we image, let go of logic.

BUBBLES

See yourself with a jar of bubble liquid and ring for blowing bubbles...dip into the jar and blow one small bubble...watch as it floats into the air...now repeat that act as you blow five more bubbles...count them as you go...pop each of the bubbles...next try a string of bubbles by waving your arm through the air...experiment with different sizes of bubbles...(Pause 30 seconds.)...Now it's time to blow a very large one...slowly watch it growing...as big as a basketball...dribble it along the floor and shoot at an imaginary basket...catch it and continue to make it bigger...as large as you are...feel how smooth the sides are...lift it in the air and bring it back down...get into the bubble...and float inside it into the air...observe what things look like from the inside of a bubble...notice whether you can hear anything...get the bubble to take you back down again...step out...and make the bubble smaller...and smaller...put it in a safe place...when I count to 5, open your eyes...1...2...3...4...5.

Processing Out

Was there anyone who had difficulty with this image? (Too much logic, i.e. the bubble broke, I couldn't make it big enough, etc.) Did anyone feel playful during the exercise? (This is usual for a creative exercise.) Did you feel relaxed? (This is expected by this time, thus the longer count at the end. The counting of bubbles at the beginning and the idea of floating should also help in achieving a relaxed state.) Did you have any trouble controlling the bubble? (This is a new component and will be exercised more in later activities. It is essential that the imager have control of the images, whether it means stopping an unwanted image, allowing an interfering image to pass by and get "back to business," or simply "playing" with the images. Assure students that this ability will come with practice.) Did you experience anything else that you'd like to share? (Accept all responses. Don't try to analyze.)

Teacher Notes

Many stories have illustrations that represent IMAGINATION IMAGES. Ask students to locate one and share it with the class, discussing how it does or does not seem to be an accurate interpretation of the story. Can they find any that trigger their own imaginations just by looking at them? Have students watch a cartoon with the sound turned down. Then discuss how cartoons are the result of an imagination image in the mind of the cartoonist.

You may even wish to begin the lesson by actually blowing bubbles outside and observing them. Not only would this be an enjoyable way to begin the lesson, but it will emphasize the ''playful'' nature of IMAGINATION IMAGES.

PLEASANT EXPERIENCES

Purpose

To develop an awareness of the senses and their importance in the imagery process.

Materials

Student page, "Multi-sensory Clustering," (Teachers may also wish to make a similar transparency from the student page, on which to demonstrate, rather than at the board.)

Procedure

We've seen how MEMORY images can bring with them strong emotional responses. When an event is stored in your memory, the right side of your brain also records the information brought to it through your senses. This is the reason why merely an odor, or sound, or taste, or touch can trigger a vivid image of something from your past. (This includes books read, movies viewed, dreams and actual experiences as well.) The more aware we are of the multisensory impressions that obviously belong to the experience, the greater the chance that we can recreate that experience in the reader's mind's eye.

(Project the student page or simply draw it on the board.)

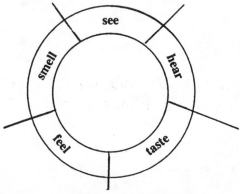

Figure 4-1

We'll use this diagram to collect our sensory impressions of "A Day at the Beach" (Write, "a day at the beach," in the center circle. Then divide the class into 5 groups and assign a "sense" to each. Allow 3 minutes for the group to brainstorm things that they might experience through whatever sense they have been given during a day at the beach. At the end of the time, ask a spokesperson from each group to write in several of their ideas. If a transparency is used, you may wish to write them in, circulating between groups as they brainstorm. The finished diagram may look like this:

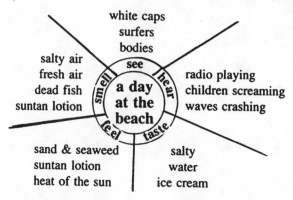

Figure 4-2

34

Notice that the word "feel" may be interpreted in two ways. As you read the sensory impressions, do you also begin to image a day at the beach? Is there any sense that seems to be dominant? (Accept all responses.) Now on a piece of paper, list 5 pleasant experiences that you have had, or enjoy doing any time. You will not have to read these aloud. (With this age group, there will certainly be sexual references or at least boy-girl relationships inferred. Try to place the focus on the process, not the content. They must feel comfortable with these strong images, not try to hide them or replace them with superficial ones. Once they have dealt with them, they will be able to move on to others.) When you have finished, select one and write it in the center of the circle. (Distribute student page or simply have them draw their own from the board example.) *Now, close your eyes for a minute, and recall that experience, paying attention to what could be seen...(pause 10 seconds)...heard...felt...tasted...and smelled...scan the entire scene...feel the pleasantness of it...when you feel ready, open your eyes and complete your diagram.*

Processing Out

Which images were more vivid, the ones that occurred when you listed the pleasant experiences or when you closed your eyes and viewed each sensory component? (Adding details aids the vividness component. Taking time to focus also will add richness to the total picture.) Did anyone get a definite dominant emotional feeling as they filled in the diagram? This is probably the same feeling that you would want a reader to experience as they are drawn into the writing. Of course they will also bring to it their own memory images, and so it will never be exactly the same for any two people. Was there any sense that seemed to be difficult for you to experience in your mind's eye? (Smell and taste are often mentioned.)

Teacher Notes

This activity is similar to the multi-sensory clustering activities that can be found in the next section. You may wish to try some of those after doing this.

MULTI-SENSORY IMAGES

Purpose

To allow students to experience all of the senses during an imagery exercise. (You may not wish to do all of the ones given. Select at least 2 so there is some basis for comparison during the processing out.)

Materials

("Multi-sensory Clustering," student page, may be used.)

Procedure

I am going to ask you to close your eyes and image several different foods through all of your senses. It is not important that you like all of the foods. Just become aware of the total picture and feeling it generates.

SODA

Close your eyes and see a can of soda...notice the color of the label...read it...now, slowly pop the top and listen to the rush of air...put your lips to the opening and feel the fizzling soda against them...take a long slow drink...feel it going into your mouth...and down your throat...notice the taste of the soda...and the smell...feel the cold can in your fingers...When I count to three, open your eyes...1...2...3.

Would anyone like to share anything about that image?

HOT CHOCOLATE

Close your eyes and see a mug of piping hot chocolate...it has a mound of whipped cream on the top...gently pick up the mug...feel how warm and heavy it feels...smell the chocolaty steam coming up through the whipped cream...watch as some of the cream melts into the hot chocolate...taste the cream...blow across the top of the mug to cool it off...and take a sip...feel the warm liquid going all the way down to your stomach...take one more sip...when I count to three, open your eyes...1...2...3.

Would anyone like to share what they imaged?

FAVORITE FRUIT

Close your eyes and see your favorite fruit...examine the shades of color...look for any imperfections...feel the texture of the skin gently...notice the weight of the fruit...slice down into it with a knife...feeling the texture of the inside parts as you cut...feel the juice on your fingers...and taste it...examine the inside of the fruit...smell its sweetness...now take a slow bite, savoring the taste...enjoy the fruit...when I count to three, open your eyes...1...2...3.

Is there anyone who wants to share their experience? (If using the student page, "Multi-sensory Clustering," have students complete the page before discussion begins.)

Processing Out

(Ask these questions after you have done at least 2 of the exercises.) What senses were the easiest to image? Which were still difficult? Think back to the most vivid image that you had. Why do you think it was so vivid? (Some may just have had that food and it is still in their short-term memory. Some may like one food over another. If the first image was especially strong, it may have forced a block on the second one. If the second was stronger, it may be due to the increased relaxation time. Probably the room was much more still and "centered" on the second try.) Is there anyone who feels that their sensory awareness is increasing during the imagery? Do you notice anything else happening? (Hopefully, relaxation, vividness and trust during these exercises are also developing.)

Teacher Notes

Since advertising uses multi-sensory imagery, you may want to ask students to observe radio, T.V. and magazine ads with respect to their appeal to the senses. Discuss how a visual picture can trigger taste, touch, etc. Teachers may also ask students to actually experience eating something and then write about it in the first person/present tense. Students could also be assigned to write about eating a piece of fruit before and after the imagery exercise, comparing both at the end.

GUIDED FANTASY

A PICNIC

Purpose

To guide students through an imagery experience that incorporates both memory and imagination.

Materials

None.

Procedure

I would like you to sit comfortably and relax. Close your eyes and see yourself carrying a large picnic basket...you are walking down a sunny, grassy path...feel the warmth of the sun...smell the fresh air...pick a place to spread out your blanket...notice the color of the blanket...and how it feels...as you flatten it out on the ground...now stretch out on your back...get comfortable...listen to a bird in a tree branch above you...examine its color...the softness of the feathers...OBSERVE what it's doing...(long pause)...now feel yourself getting hungry...open the basket and take out your favorite food...smell it...enjoy eating it...(long pause)...quench your thirst with something from the basket...scan the setting around you as you get ready to explore...see something interesting in the distance and begin to move toward it, slowly...try to figure out what it is as it becomes more and more clear to you...use all of your senses to understand it better...(pause 1-2 minutes)...now return to your blanket as I count to ten...1...2...3...4...5...prepare to come back to the room...6...7...8...9...10...open your eyes.

Processing Out

Would anyone like to share what they did or did not see? What parts of the experience were something from your memory? from your imagination? Did you feel that you had enough time to experience all that you wanted to see? (This can help you to know if you are pacing the suggestions adequately or need to allow for more time.)

Teacher Notes

If you feel that the students need more experience with guided fantasies, you may wish to use others provided in this book, (see TABLE OF CONTENTS), refer to those found in *200 Ways of Using Imagery in the Classroom*, Bagley & Hess, (see BIBLIOGRAPHY) or write some of your own using the guidelines provided.

CHANGING AND CONTROLLING IMAGES

Purpose

To practice controlling the image as well as changing, (transforming) its color, shape, size or use.

Materials

None.

Procedure

We're going to use our imaginations to change what is now in the room. You do not have to close your eyes, but please do not talk while imaging.

Look around the room and see it as it is now...see your classmates in their seats...change the school seats to more comfortable ones...make them soft, cushiony easy chairs...make all of the chairs blue...put on music that you'd like to be listening to...turn it up loudly...see everyone getting up to dance...make the chairs disappear...feel the beat of the music...see the floor become a dance floor...remove the walls...make the room much, much bigger...change the floor to sand...look out at the ocean...see picnic baskets, beach umbrellas, radios, towels and blankets...see a large rain cloud...watch everyone run for cover...back to the classroom.

Processing Out

Would anyone like to share what they did or did not image? (Accept all answers.) Which senses were easiest to use? Let's list the kinds of changes you had to make during the activity (type of seat, color of seat, feeling of seat, remove seats, hear music, change volume of music, move people, color of floor, texture of floor, remove walls, bring in new objects, etc.). You don't realize, perhaps, that you had to shift so many times during the activity. Don't worry if you could not see everything. It takes practice to be able to control and change your images. This could be the most important skill that you develop. The more you use the skill, the more refined it will become.

Teacher Notes

For practice, you may want to have the students go home and sit in their bedrooms, rearranging the furniture, mentally. Tell them that they may also add new objects to their rooms...money is no concern! When they have planned out the ideal room, have them draw a floorplan of it. This exercise will be fun and good practice in change and control.

This is a good lead-up exercise to THE WORKSHOP which can be found at the end of this section and CONTROLLABILITY.

CONTROLLABILITY

Purpose

To explore the components of controlling images: (a) summoning an image at will, (b) stopping an image when desired, (c) moving an image in space in order to see it from different vantage points.

Materials

None.

PART I

Procedure

We are going to combine both memory and imagination in this activity. I would like you to first close your eyes and sit in a comfortable position. For the next 30 seconds I would like you to see your bedroom at home...noticing the furniture...fabrics and colors...and any special possessions that you have there...(allow for at least 30 seconds after the last suggestion). Now open your eyes when you feel that you have a clear picture and make a simple sketch of that room as if you are looking down at it from the ceiling. (This should not take more than 5 minutes. If they wish to label items, they may. These need not be shared with the class. As they are finishing, ask these discussion questions:) Did anyone have trouble seeing his room? (Probably not, since this involves both short and long-term memory. Students who did not see anything were not relaxed or perhaps have some negative feelings tied to the image of their room and did not allow themselves to see it. Accept all responses without probing the reasons. They may still be able to do the second part of the exercise.) What things were especially vivid? (Usually things that bring pleasure, such as a phone, stereo, new clothes, records or furniture will be mentioned. Point out the feeling tied to the images. It will also show in the body language used while students share their images.) Was anyone in the room? (Some may see parents, siblings, friends or themselves in the room.) Did you reimage your room while you were drawing the floorplan? (Most students will say that they did. Some will even say that they saw more the second time. This is because they have already focused on and developed the image, making it easier to go back to, and also to add details.) Did you image anything that you did not expect to? (Imagination can be responsible for this if it involves something that could "never" happen. Memory, on the other hand, can recall aspects of a former bedroom or an object long forgotten. Accept all responses.)

PART II

Procedure

Now that you have created the image of your room in your mind's eye, I am going to ask you to go back to that image and see it from different vantage points. Once you have done that, I will ask you to remodel your room in any way that you wish. Stretch your ability to be creative and see what happens. *Get into a comfortable position and relax. Listen to your breathing as it becomes steady and quiet. Close your eyes and go back to your room...stand in the middle of the room and turn slowly so that*

40

you can scan each wall...rise above the room and see it from the ceiling...notice the tops of everything...now go out of the room and look in through a window or door...observe what can be seen and make a note of what cannot be seen from here...now have some fun with the furniture...rearrange it...or change it to something you prefer in its place...if you need more room, change the size of the room...or the shape...or the construction...(pauses should be at least 20 seconds from now on)...create the perfect room for you...use your favorite colors...play your favorite music...invite a friend in to see it...give a tour of your room...listen to the reaction of your friend...show it to someone in your family...listen to what they say about it...enjoy being in it...as I count to ten, become more aware of yourself in the classroom...1...2...3...4...5...6...7...8...9...10...open your eyes.

Processing Out

Would anyone like to share anything about this image? Were you able to go back to the image of what your room really looks like more easily than you were at the beginning of class? Were you able to stop the image of the real room when it was time to rearrange and change it? Were you able to see the real room from different views? (Assure the students that these abilities will develop with practice and will come more easily as they continue to trust the imaging process and let go of logic.)

Teacher Notes

If you feel that a great deal of practice is needed, you may wish to do more guided fantasies before going on. It does not take too long before all students have some ability to control mental images. Here is a suggestion for a shorter exercise in controllability:

See an apple...make it red...change it to green...now make it yellow...change it to a lemon...and then an orange...draw lines on it so it looks like a basketball...use a pump to inflate it...bounce it...pop it like a balloon...open your eyes.

You can adapt the above exercise to shoes, animals, cars, or any object at all. The students can be asked to write a short imagery exercise in controllability using the one above as a model. Just creating this will be good practice for them. Have them include changes in color, size, shape and type of objects imaged as well as moving the objects in some way. This exercise could be the beginning script for a flip book or short animated film. Direct the students to be aware of T.V. commercials that use animation to change visual images; there are many.

VIVIDNESS

Purpose

To demonstrate to the students how the eye continually refocuses in order to achieve a vivid image. Once understood, similar mental focussing can be accomplished.

ACTIVITY #1

Materials

None.

Procedure

I would like you to hold up your hand, at arm's length, in front of your face. Look at your hand. Keep looking at your hand and try to see what is beyond it. Can you get a clear picture of your hand? of the background? Now look past your hand to get a vivid picture of the background. Keep looking at the background and try to see your hand clearly. Put your hand down now and tell me what you discovered. (The eyes can only focus on close or far at one time. They must be shifting all day long in order to see what's happening. Students who wear glasses may also mention that this is the reason they only wear glasses for certain tasks. Bifocal lenses were invented for just this reason.) The mind's eye can do the same type of refocusing to make an image become clear.

ACTIVITY #2

Materials

Picture File, OUT-OF-FOCUS pictures, (see APPENDIX).

Procedure

Look at the picture that I've given you, (or projected onto the screen). Pretend that you are looking through a camera lens at it. Slowly use your mind's eye to bring it into focus...closing your own eyes as you make the picture more vivid. See the picture as clearly as you can. Notice every detail. (pause) Scan the scene and snap the shutter at just the right moment. (pause) And then open your eyes.

Processing Out

What did you take a picture of? (When the entire class uses the same picture, it is most interesting to share answers.) Did the color seem to guide your thoughts? What do you think would happen if it were black and white? All black? All white? All of any color? (The imagination would become active. For example, white would become, perhaps, a soft baby harp seal on an iceberg during a snowstorm.)

Teacher Notes

A very easy writing activity using the blur as a beginning, is to have students write a brief description of the clear picture, using details that they imaged. These can be hung on a bulletin board next to the OUT-OF-FOCUS pictures, written or typed onto an OUT-OF-FOCUS picture, or using water colors, create their own OUT-OF-FOCUS pictures. Photography students can develop some of those ''rejected'' shots that actually were out of focus and use them.

The writing may be in any form. I like to use a formula that gives a poetic feeling to the piece. Artistic types of lettering will also enhance the poetic flow. Here are a few formulas that you may wish to use:

Formula	Student Example
Line #1: Object/noun	A chameleon
Line #2: Describe noun	Bright, scintillating
Line #3: Place the noun	In the red, yellow and orange fall leaves
Line #4: Give it action	Slowly looking for something.
	—Pietro Michelucci (Gr. 9)
Line #1: Name a feeling or emotion	Calm
Line #2: ''is'' + verb	is sleeping
Line #3: Setting	in a crystal, rainbow room.
	—Chris Rafferty (Gr. 5)

Watching/observing smoke, mist, clouds, bubbles, frost, fog, the sky, leaves moving, lights, shadows, water, rain, sleet, snow, moving traffic, moving scenery as you pass, clay as you work it, paint as you mix it, wood as you sand it, and many other daily activities and happenings while allowing your mind the freedom to form mental pictures of things that the imagination wants to see is a wonderful way to exercise your skill of vividness and create a calmness within.

AFTER-IMAGES

Purpose

To introduce the concept of after-images and how they are different from memory and imagination images.

Materials

Transparencies, "After-images" (APPENDIX) prepared according to the directions.

Procedure

We have all experienced "seeing the flash" after a picture has been taken and many have also watched a bolt of lightning against a dark sky, reappear after the initial flash. Today we're going to examine that phenomenon.

(Project the white circle on the dark background.) Focus your eyes on the dot in the circle. Try not to look away or blink. (Count 30 seconds, then pull the transparency away quickly.) Keep looking at the screen and tell me what you see. (At first they will see the white circle, then it will reverse to a dark circle on white.)

(Next project the dark circle on white and give the same instructions. This time the after-image becomes a white circle.) If dark becomes light and light becomes dark, what do you think will happen with colors? (Some may guess that complementary colors will be seen as the after-images, but let them test *any* theory that is suggested.)

(Project the RED circle, the BLUE and the YELLOW in the same manner. You may wish to repeat if there seems to be disagreement. Turn off the overhead projector during each discussion to give the eyes a rest. You may wish to record the findings on the chalkboard after each discussion.)

Processing Out

Why is the after-image called a negative image? Can you scan an after-image? (No. The image moves with your eyes. You may want to do one more just to try it.) Can you see any kind of details or just the shape and color? (Suggest that they try using a 3-dimensional object against a white background, an apple, toy, cup or glass, etc.) Do you control seeing the after-image or does it just happen and then go away? How are after-images different from memory and imagination images? Can you re-image, or call back an after-image? (When staring at a circle, the retina becomes saturated with the image and produces an after-image. It is more an experience of sight than of seeing with the mind's eye.)

THE WORKSHOP

Purpose

To allow students to create a mental working atmosphere where their creativity and self-confidence can grow and become productive.

Materials

None.

Procedure

You are going to build a workshop—a place that is safe, relaxing and magical. Here you will have all that you need to solve problems, prepare for coming events in your life or try out new ideas. Nothing is impossible in your workshop. You may go there or change it to suit your needs at any time. It is yours and yours alone; only you control what happens there. Get into a comfortable position and relax...See yourself beginning to build the floor of your workshop...Use whatever you wish and make it exactly the way you want it...(pause 1 minute)...When you finish the floors, begin constructing the walls, using any textures or colors that suit you...(pause 1 minute)...Put things on the walls that you enjoy looking at...When the walls and floor are finished, scan the room and make any changes that you feel are necessary...(pause 1 minute)...Next build the ceiling, paying attention to lighting and anything else you see as a part of it...Observe what you've built so far...Now it's time to furnish your workshop. Make it fit your tastes. Make it comfortable and homey...(pause 2 minutes)...Relax in a comfortable spot and scan your workshop. Notice every detail...Change anything that you wish to improve...Now add a place where you can write down ideas...next place a movie screen somewhere. You will need it for future problem solving...See a door opening and watch as two close friends enter. They are supportive of you and will always be available when you need their advice or assistance. Invite them in for a short visit...(pause 2 minutes)...It's time now to say good-bye to your friends...Scan the workshop one more time while I count to ten...1...2...3...4...5...6...7...8...9...10...Open your eyes.

Processing Out

Would anyone like to share his experience? Did the furnishings fit your personal tastes? Was it a place that you could feel comfortable in? Was there anything you had trouble doing? (Some students may not want to put the screen or writing desk into their workshops yet. They are not ready to work in the workshop. When they accept the workshop as a place to get ideas, they will be ready to work there.) Did you see your friends clearly? (Some may be surprised by who entered the workshop. It may not be a "pal" from their usual peer group, but rather a parent, teacher, historical figure, rock star or even someone who has died or moved away. Let them know that there must be a reason for that person being there or their mind would not have suggested him. They can always control who enters their workshop and if there is someone they wish to keep out, that's okay. Other students may wish to work alone Remind them, once again have complete control over it.)

Teacher Notes

Don't be shocked by *anything* that they have in their workshops. It is important that you accept their control over individual ideas. Do not judge or press them to share what is in their workshop. Students must feel that they really do have complete control. Eventually positive thoughts will emerge.

You may wish to have students draw a floorplan of their workshop to reinforce the images that they experienced. Drawings, of course, can be revised at any time.

"But how will I know if the pictures I see are the right ones?" the boy asked.

"If they come from within then they are the right ones," answered the man.

—The Karate Kid

CHAPTER FIVE

Introductory Writing Activities

During the process of writing the emphasis should be on ideas—not mechanics. That is not to say that the mechanics are not important. Indeed, they are essential if we are to communicate our good ideas to others, but it is necessary to develop creative ideas *before* worrying about polishing and sharing them. I tell students to first be a writer then be an editor. This reinforces the idea that there are several steps in the writing process and focusing on one at a time is much more effective than trying to do everything at once. It also means that the teacher should not "rush" the process. Time spent on experimentation, incubation and elaboration of ideas can make the difference between mediocre and magnificent writing.

The primary purpose of the Introductory Writing Activities is to get students to begin to look at writing as a creative act rather than a technical skill. Students say that they cannot write when what they really mean to say is that they cannot put creative ideas into written form while they are overly concerned with the technical and mechanical aspects of writing. Where did they get this attitude? From an educational system that rarely rewards and reinforces creativity but always evaluates writing on the basis of correct spelling, punctuation and form. If you have heard students asking, "Does spelling count?" or "How long does this have to be?" then you can be sure that there are already limits being set that will hinder, if not eliminate a creative flow of ideas.

You must begin to get back that love of words that all children experienced before entering school. The best way that I know to do that is to allow students to once again become storytellers. Let them have and share creative ideas. Let them enjoy language. Let them take risks and be outrageous once in a while! Everyone wants to feel successful at writing. What better way to encourage success than to encourage individuality and creative thought?

Each time I teach my writing course, the graduate students (mostly teachers) make it very clear to me and to the rest of the class that they cannot write, have never been able to write well (even some of the English teachers) and really only expect to get some good ideas to use with their students. This is why they take the course. I smile, knowing where the course will lead them. As gently as possible, I tell them that the course requirement is writing...lots of it...poems, conversations, play scripts, short stories, etc. After the gasps subside, I smile and begin the introductory writing activities. And do you know what happens? Long before we get to number ten, most have forgotten that they ever said they they couldn't write; some are totally baffled by the fact that it's coming so easily; and everyone is having a wonderful time with the English language—writing it, reading it, and hearing it being read. This, to me, is the very essence of writing—the pleasure that comes from knowing that your ideas are worth sharing. This is what gives writing purpose.

The Introductory Writing Activities are organized in the sequence that I have found to be most successful. Whether or not you follow the suggested order or do all of the activities is not important. You know best what your needs are and should use this section as a guide to getting started. Probably you will want to modify them to suit your time schedule, grade level and students' abilities. (You may wish to note that each of the later sections of the book begins with a few simple warm-up activities, so you may decide to skip to another section after just trying a couple of these.) Don't be hesitant to use the activities because they appear to be too simple, too elementary or too "cute" for high school students. It's true that they can easily be used with younger students, but that's because they are intended to be nonthreatening—almost inviting. The best testimony to this is what teachers write to tell me after they've tried some of the activities. Here are some excerpts from their letters:

"There are so many wonderful writing ideas, I've hardly begun to assimilate all of them. I've done several with my classes and they love writing this way," (Penny Miller)

"Enclosed are some samples of writing that I did with my students recently. These activities have become so enjoyable that my students are now clamoring for a Writing Workshop time." (Nancy Materese)

"I plunged headlong into using your methods, and my kids and I are having a pretty glorious time. My walls are plastered with decorated acrostic poetry, and I have won several bets against some young men who vociferously insisted that I could not get them to write poetry. In one class we found 49 different ways to say 'no', and tomorrow we are going to see how rich the English language is when it comes to saying 'yes.' (The bets are not nearly as rich.) In my slowest non-regent class we have written ten "I used to be but now..,"'s (and it took two days) and today they chose one and wrote a paragraph about how the change took place. As a tangential benefit, the sharing of assignments has led some closet poets to share some personal writing with me—and I have some very talented though shy students on every ability level. Only one lone student has accused me of making the room look like a kindergarten classroom with all of its pictures and creative projects. The rest seem quietly pleased. Me too!" (Wendy Dembeck, 10th grade teacher)

All writing activities should be presented in an non-threatening manner because it is this attitude that will break down the barriers. Once the writing has been completed, students can begin to polish their writing. This may be done individually, in small or large groups, or with a mentor or teacher. There are many suggestions in the POLISH TO PUBLISH section near the end of the book which you may wish to skim through just before beginning and incorporate into the process in a non-judgmental way. Below are some brief comments about the Introductory Writing Activities.

Activities #1&2

Often the first spoken word, "no" is a word of many meanings. For these reasons, the first activity explores the many different ways to say "no." Then, after the realization that our perceptions determine interpretations of the written and spoken word, the second activity forces students to be selective of the words that they use to communicate their intended meanings. These first two exercises point out to students the importance of the words used in their writing, that using trite words and phrases can lead to misinterpretations and although it might take some creative energy, selecting the "right" word or words is what will set their writing apart from everyone else's.

Activity #3

Sharing is important to writing because it allows readers to get feedback about clarity, encouragement to continue developing creative ideas, and a "feeling" for the rhythms and recurrences in their writing. Group writing takes away the ownership of writing so that students can experience writing and sharing as a positive rather than a negative activity. Other ways to encourage sharing may include:
—suggesting that the students take pen names which are only known to the teacher
—collecting unsigned work, mixing it up and redistributing it to the members of the class to be read aloud
—collecting written work and reading it to the class without revealing the author's name.
I have found that once students see the value of sharing their work in an atmosphere where the emphasis is not on evaluation, they become comfortable and even welcome that step in the process.

Activities #4,5,6

The use of cartoons, pictures and word cards gives writing a starting point with many possible directions. Students soon recognize that their personal input is an integral part of the writing and are usually anxious to get started when they know that there is freedom within the given guidelines. The additional benefit of using these motivational aids is that students learn to get ideas for writing from many different sources, and soon begin to design their own writing activities. It is just as effective to teach the writing of essays, vignettes, articles, arguments or short stories while allowing personal interests and humor to be incorporated into them, as not. The only difference will be that students will actually enjoy writing and be more willing to write even when they don't have to! Using non-threatening methods to introduce a new writing skill places the focus on the skill instead of on both the skill and the content. Once the skill has been mastered, have students move on to more challenging content.

Activity #7

If each piece of writing that a student does is to be rewritten several times, read aloud, or published for the class and evaluated by the teacher, then students might just get the idea that there is no such thing as writing for the sake of writing. It will always be something that's been assigned and results in a grade. Free writing is a wonderful way to get away from the evaluative nature of writing assignments. It gives students a chance to analyze what they "feel" like when they write, how their minds work to connect and elaborate on their thoughts and what kind of ideas come out when they tap inner resources.

Activities #8 & 9

Prewriting activities are vital to good writing yet we teachers, because of the demands on us to cover curriculum and prepare for standardized testing, often eliminate this step or at best, minimize the time spent on the "gathering" of ideas. I have found that clustering, (also called mind mapping or webbing) and multi-sensory clustering are extremely efficient and effective ways to prepare for writing. They can be used as "personal brainstorming" techniques, encouraging a free flow of ideas while putting them into an organized and useable format. Clustering and multi-sensory clustering are just as effective for poetry as prose and have been used successfully (with modifications) by both young children and adults. These techniques heighten the integrative powers of the mind, producing harmony between the right and left hemispheres.

Clustering can also be used in teaching study skills: note-taking being the initial step of gathering information about a topic, outlining the topic by organizing the notes of each branch into a subtopic and writing a report or speech from the outline. A perfect example of clustering used in this way is what I did to prepare to write this book. I had hundreds of unorganized activities and really didn't know where to put them all. I simply wrote "creative writing book" in the center of a large page and began to draw branches from the center. Each time an idea popped into my head I skimmed to see where best to "attach" it. If there was a "stray" idea that appeared to belong nowhere, I simply wrote it in a circle at the outer edge of the page and connected it at a later time. As I searched other books and tried new exercises, I simply continued to add to the cluster until I felt that the "note-taking step" had been completed. From this I wrote my first outline, each subtopic (or major branch) becoming one of the sections of the book. I then clustered each subtopic individually. This helped me to combine similar activities, eliminate unnecessary ones and select a sequence. From that point, the writing was easy—or at least organized!

Activity #10

Wanting to write their own guided fantasies is a common request from students. For this reason I have provided guidelines to make it easy and to avoid problems. The problems that I refer to are the potentially unpleasant experiences that can result from a "scary" imagery exercise. These may contain suggestions that take the imager up into the air or under water, for example. Although the author isn't bothered by the words, there may be a classmate who is fearful of heights or water and will become upset during the imagery exercise. Since I never know what to expect when it comes to group imaging, I take the following steps as a precaution:

—Continually reinforce the idea that the imager has control during imagery and can end an unpleasant reaction by opening the eyes.

—Keep a watchful eye on the class during imagery. If a student seems disturbed, interject a statement such as , "remember that you are in control at all times" or "you are safe from harm and can return to the classroom at will." Keep your voice tone calm and approach the student, gently touching a shoulder or arm.

—Before beginning an imagery with the class, mention where they will be "going." I will kiddingly ask if anyone is afraid of flying, etc. and if so would rather not do this one.

—When students write their own guided fantasies, I sometimes put them on a transparency or large chart for all to see. We then go over them together, making modifications if needed before they are read as imagery exercises.

All of the above are simply to make you more aware of ways to insure a successful lesson. The negative reactions are few and far between, and for me have never been worse than unpleasant. Going slowly and maintaining a warm rapport with students is the best advice that I can give you. The rewards, people learning to like themselves better and in turn liking and respecting others more, are so worthwhile that that is where your energy should be focussed.

(1) NO!

Purpose

To introduce to students the idea of how many different ways there are to say the same thing.

Procedure

Write the word "NO" on the blackboard and ask students to suggest different ways to write the word "no." Explain that they may use punctuation marks, change the size of the letters, etc. to indicate their own personal interpretations. When someone gets an idea, hand him the chalk and have him write it at the board. (I have that student pass the chalk to another. The next student has the option of writing or passing the chalk. Allow the chalk to circulate the room *at least* two times. This allows for extended "think time" to generate new ideas.) Eventually some students will ask if they may use phrases, foreign words, etc. Of course, let them! Fill the board!

Processing Out

Discuss the following:
  —Why were we able to come up with so many different ways to say "no?"
  —Does the situation dictate which word or words were used?
  —In writing, does your choice of words make a difference?

Follow-up Activity

In small groups, brainstorm other ways to say: please, yes, thank you, beautiful, good, nice, great, etc.
  —In small groups, brainstorm words with multiple meanings. These can be listed on a chart as a reminder that there are many ways to say the same thing.
  —Use the list on the blackboard to write an essay on "How to Say No."

(2) ONE-WORD CONVERSATIONS

Purpose

To force students to be selective about the words they use in order to convey a specific meaning. To use as few words as possible while communicating.

Procedure

Students select partners and work in pairs. Instruct them that student A will speak one word and student B will respond with one word. Student A again speaks one word and the process continues until "Time's Up!" is called. At no time may either student speak more than one word. To help give a focus, you may wish to add one of these instructions:
—Student A find out what student B did last weekend or would like to have done.
—Student A find out about a vacation that student B took or would like to take.
—Student A discover something "new" about student B such as a career ambition or hobby.
When "Time's Up" is called (usually after one minute) students A and B can reverse roles.

Processing Out

Discuss general comments about the activity, then ask:
—Did the focusing instructions make it easier to converse?
—Was it difficult to use only one word? How did you decide which word to use when you wanted to use more?

Follow-up Activity

—Play a game to review stories read by the class. You state for example, the theme and they respond (using one word), the character, part of the title, or author's name.
—Make a cartoon strip depicting dialogue between two characters from a story or historical event. Use only one word each time a character speaks.
—Select pictures from ads, etc. and write one-word captions that sum up the main idea.

(3) GROUP WRITING

Purpose

To encourage creative thoughts in writing and oral reading of that writing in a non-threatening manner.

Procedure

Each student takes out a blank sheet of paper and writes the words, "The ————", filling in the blank with a noun. Instruct each student to fold the paper over, hiding what was written (I sometimes suggest using a paper clip to keep it folded) and pass it to another student. This procedure continues in the same manner for the rest of the writing.

—Line #2—Write 3 adjectives that could describe the hidden noun. Fold and pass.
—Line #3—Write a verb phrase telling what the unknown noun is doing. Fold and pass.
—Line #4—Write a phrase describing how it's doing it. Fold and pass.
—Line #5—Write a phrase that tells where it's being done. Fold and pass.
—Line #6—Write a phrase telling when the action is taking place.

After the sixth person has written his line, instruct each to unfold the paper, read silently (make sure to allow for laughter), edit it so it can be read orally and read it aloud to the class.

Processing Out

Discuss why reading these orally was not embarrassing to anyone.
Discuss the value of reading orally.
Discuss the visual images evoked when each was read aloud.

Follow-up Activity

—Begin with the words, "The teacher" (if you're brave) and continue with the instructions above.
—Rearrange the instructions or write new ones and repeat the activity.
—Try the activity without the folding, but passing the paper for each new line to be added.
—Choose a category, such as "Famous People" or "Book Titles" and follow the "no folding" rule.
—After reading aloud, use the information to write a short story, elaborating on each line.

Teacher's Note

To keep this activity running smoothly, you may wish to call out, "fold and pass" at the appropriate times.

(4) USING CARTOONS

Purpose

To use the non-threatening format of cartoons to stimulate creative writing.

Materials

CARTOON ACTIVITY CARDS (APPENDIX) See directions below for making additional cards.

Procedure

Give each student enough time to read over and select a CARTOON ACTIVITY CARD. Have them follow directions on the card, doing the required writing. After editing takes place, students may wish to redraw (or even trace—that's okay, too) the cartoon as an illustration for their writing. Display the finished products.

Follow-up Activity

—Have students select another card and write according to the directions on it.
—Have students work in groups to make additional CARTOON ACTIVITY CARDS (See directions below.)
—Have students make up writing activities for other pictures as well.

Making Additional Cartoon Activity Cards

1. Save the colored comic section from Sunday newspapers for several weeks.
2. Select and cut individual cartoon boxes that are ''interesting looking,'' simple to draw or show a scene related to writing, such as Snoopy at the typewriter, or Linus writing to the Great Pumpkin.
3. Using one or two of these boxes for each activity card, brainstorm as many possible writing ideas as you can and print them on a piece of construction paper or oaktag. You may also wish to cut out the words from the ''balloons,'' suggesting new dialogue as part of the activity.
4. Glue on the cartoon boxes and laminate or cover with clear contact paper to extend the life of the card.

Teacher's Note

Some activities should be shorter and easier than others for those students who are reluctant to write. Remember, even writing a list and correcting spelling mistakes should be considered a writing activity. Some students would rather begin with two short easy activities than one longer one. I usually set a time limit for writing so that when one activity is completed another one can be started and all students put in equal time, even though it may mean ½ card for one student and 2 cards for another.

(5) PICTURE/WORD SYNTHESIS

Purpose

To write meaningful captions for pictures and to explore multiple meanings of words.

Materials

Picture File (APPENDIX) and 3x5 cards.

Procedure

Have students each select a picture from the picture file. Instruct each student to write a caption for the picture using a predetermined vocabulary word. (This could come from a Spelling or vocabulary list, a newspaper headline or randomly selected from one of the texts. *All* students use the same word but different pictures.) Captions are written on 3x5 cards and can be tacked under the pictures on the bulletin board after being read aloud. (Allow students to add prefixes or suffixes if needed).

Processing Out

Discuss the following:
—How does the picture determine the word's usage?
—How does the sharing of the variety of uses help you to remember the word's meaning?
—What surprised you most about the activity?

Follow-up Activity

—Leave pictures on the bulletin board but replace 3x5 cards each day, using a new word.
—Reverse the rules, having all students describe the same picture while using different words. For further extension, then group students to write a short story together, using the picture and each one's word and caption idea.
—Have students randomly select one picture and one word and write a vignette using the word as part of the title.

Teacher's Note

Allow students to explore both fantasy and realistic interpretations. Invite humor!

(6) WORD SYNTHESIS

Purpose

To use a given set of words to create a meaningful sentence or paragraph.

Materials

WORD CARDS (APPENDIX)

Procedure

Distribute one WORD CARD to each student and give instructions to use the word in a sentence. When finished, pair students and again instruct them to write, this time, using both words. Next, form groups of four and create a new sentence or sentences using all four words. Have a spokesperson from each group read the final writing.

Processing Out

Discuss the following:
—How did the final writing differ from the first four sentences written?
—How did the group determine the best way to use all four words?
—How do the pre-selected words determine what will be written?

Follow-up Activity

(Done in a group or by individual students)
—Write as many different sentences as you can using the same four words.
—Use five or six words from a specific vocabulary list and tie them together in an interesting paragraph.

(7) FREE WRITING

Purpose

To encourage writing merely for the sake of experiencing the process, not for disclosure.

Procedure

Allow a minimum of 15 minutes for this activity. Tell students to write anything at all that they wish to write about. No one will read or hear what they've written so they may write freely. (The teacher should also write during this time). I like to play relaxing music during the activity and instruct students to write until the music ends. (See APPENDIX for recommended music.) Since the purpose is to write, the only rule is that they do so during the entire time. Some starters could be:

What I had for breakfast.
What emotion I'm feeling right now.
Why I like to write.
Why I don't like to write.

When the starting topic has been exhausted, students should simply start writing about something else until the time is up.

Processing Out

It is important to accept any and *all* reactions to this activity. I often say, "That's interesting. Did anyone else feel the same way?" This helps to validate whatever was experienced. This activity can be difficult for some students. Here are some discussion questions:

—Did anyone find this difficult to do?
—Did anyone find this an easy activity?
—How did you feel when I said you would not have to read what you wrote?
—Did anyone only write about one topic?
—What was the effect of the music on your writing?
—What was it like to write continuously?
—Did you ever write freely before?
—Do you think this type of writing has value?
—Would anyone like to share what they've written? (It is important to ask this in case a student feels the need to share. I often ask at the end of a session if anyone would like me to read theirs privately.)

Follow-up Activity

—Repeat this activity several times throughout the year, noting any changes in reactions to it.
—Free writing can be done on a regular basis in the form of a journal. Let students know this. There may be a student who wishes to begin a journal of his own.

(8) MULTI-SENSORY CLUSTERING

Purpose

To reinforce the importance of using sensory impressions in writing.

Materials

Picture File and student page, "Multi-Sensory Clustering" (APPENDIX)

Procedure

Each student should select a picture of a setting and have a copy of the student page. Instruct students to study the picture for details to get a "feel" for where the place is and then begin to jot down words and phrases in the SEE section that describe anything that they can see. After one minute tell students to do the same for HEAR. When they get to FEEL they may include feelings about being in this place and the "feel" of things here as well. They should continue all the way around twice, adding anything new that they think of as they go. Allow 10 minutes before continuing. (Remind students not to worry about continuity. The purpose is to get lots of images down on paper.)

Image

Skim what you've written so far and then put your pen down and close your eyes. See this place in your mind's eye...listen to the sounds around you...and the smells...and the tastes...notice how you feel in this place...(longer pause)...get a general sense or feeling about his place...(longer pause)...when you know what mood or feeling is being created, open your eyes and write *that* in the very center of your page. Add any new ideas that you'd like to add. (Wait until all are ready.)

Write

Use what you've written in the center as your title. If you've written a sentence, shorten it to become a title. Now skim your notes and underline anything that reinforces the title. For example, if your title is "Eerie" then underline anything that describes or elaborates on eeriness. These are the words and phrases that you should try to include when you begin to write. (Wait one minute). Begin your first line with the words, "I am " and complete it anyway you wish, describing what you are doing in this place. Let the mood emerge through your descriptions of things seen, heard, touched, tasted and smelled. Continue writing, using sentences (if prose) or phrases (if poetry is desired).

(Allow ample time for writing to be done and then add the final directions.) When you have finished, end with either a statement or question that restates the title. You may use the same words or words that mean the same thing. This will "tie" your vignette together, bringing the theme full circle.

FIGURE 5-1: Below is a sample of the cluster and writing done from a picture of snake coiled around a twig. You will notice that not all ideas from the cluster have been used in the writing, nevertheless, they were necessary in finding the theme.

MULTI-SENSORY CLUSTER AND VIGNETTE
By Ina Sinovoi

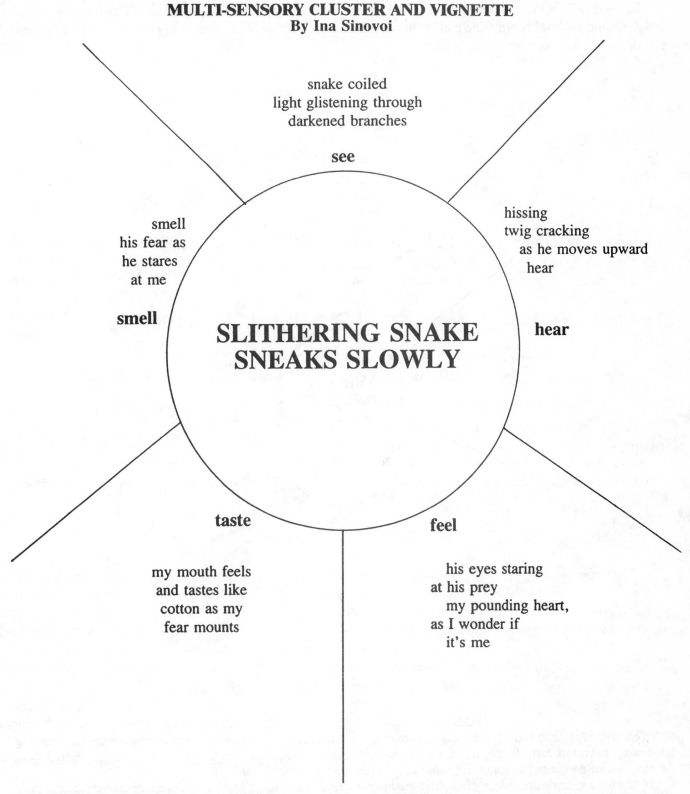

snake coiled
light glistening through
darkened branches

see

hissing
twig cracking
as he moves upward
hear

smell
his fear as
he stares
at me

smell

**SLITHERING SNAKE
SNEAKS SLOWLY**

hear

taste

feel

my mouth feels
and tastes like
cotton as my
fear mounts

his eyes staring
at his prey
my pounding heart,
as I wonder if
it's me

As I am photographing this snake slithering up the twig, the light glistens through the branches and I hear his body gliding upward, hissing loudly. I feel his eyes staring down at me. My mouth feels so dry I can hardly speak.

I smell his fear as well as my own.

FIGURE 5-2 below shows a much more detailed clustering of ideas, sparked by the picture of an old-fashioned school room. The picture was familiar to the writer, Margaret Giles and the writing became a mixture of memory and imagination.

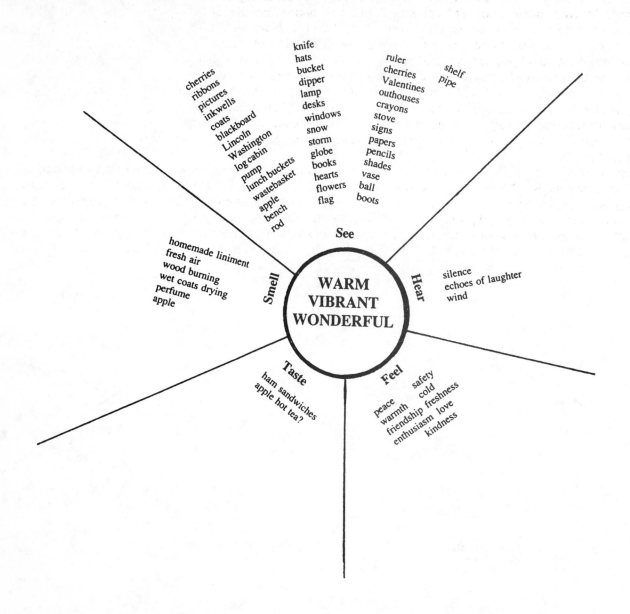

WARM, VIBRANT, WONDERFUL YESTERDAY

"You cheerful little room," Miss Clara Brown thought with a satisfied sigh as she stood in the connecting doorway between her living quarters and her literary realm. "Tiny but tidy—warm and wonderful—a small haven dedicated to learning," she continued her contented perusal.

In the background emanating from her quarters came the excited giggles and the conspiratorial whispers of her twelve pupils hastily preparing the feast. It is Valentine's Day.

"Why does it always take all five of the girls to prepare the punch?" Miss Brown wondered. "Well, even big, awkward-looking Kenneth Davis is participating this year." She smiled to herself as she pictured his large hands carefully cutting his mother's special 12-egg angel food cake.

"Yes, little room, you hold a suppressed air of excitement and tingling romance today. How happy Mary Liz will be when she sees that big heart on Marcus Kimball's desk. At seventeen and in the eighth grade, he has watched her every move all year long. I wonder how many true loves you have nurtured, little room—how many lifelong friendships."

Miss Brown surveyed the room again. "Well, the globe had certainly been shoved aside in the hurry to get on with today's more pressing business. Books and papers lay discarded on desk tops. All in all it really was a friendly room—one where everyone could feel comfortable and at ease."

The wooden wainscotting and smooth brown of the desks glowed from a recent polishing by the older girls, and the floor had been swept spotless by the boys last night in preparation for today. The bright orange of the bittersweet in the vase on her desk was a nice touch of color.

Drawing in a deep breath, Miss Brown was satisfied with the rich cedary smell of wood burning in the shining pot-bellied stove and the whiffs of clear, fresh, snowy air which pushed in around the window sills. They almost completely defeated the odor of drying wool coming from the recess-wet coats and mittens hanging in the cloak closets. There was also the lingering hint of ham sandwiches and crisp MacIntosh apples.

The kerosene lamps lit a soft glow in the late afternoon gloom, and the new water bucket and dipper echoed the glimmer. Kind Mr. Depew at the mercantile had even donated the colorful streamers so that the two great presidents could be honored properly. Yes, February seemed a cold place everywhere but in the schoolroom where the bright fire and energetic children seemed to deny that the cold even existed.

The sounds of the party again intruded on Miss Brown's reverie, and she hurried to get out the penny chocolate hearts—the ones which said, "I love you!" Her last thought before the party began was, "Please little Judith Lee, don't need to use the outhouse before the party is over."

(9) CLUSTERING

Purpose

To allow for a free flow of ideas related to a particular topic before the actual writing takes place.

Materials

Two 8-inch pieces of string and two 3x5 cards for each student.

Procedure

Arrange desks in a circle so that there's a large area of floor space easily seen by all. Select a topic or theme to write about. Some that work well for this activity are: time, freedom, maze, age, afraid, dreams or journey. (Almost any word or phrase will do.) Write the theme on a large card and place it in the center of the floor space. Ask students to think of any idea that the center word evokes and write it on their cards. One at a time, students should use the string to connect their ideas to another card on the floor. A web-like effect should occur. (See diagram). For example, if the theme is journey, one student may write "into space" and a second student might add "space shuttle" or "2001" or "lost in space." Then the idea would perhaps shift to a different type of journey—"back in time" and that would spark ideas like, "time tunnel," "time machine" or "reincarnation." So far your cluster would look like this:

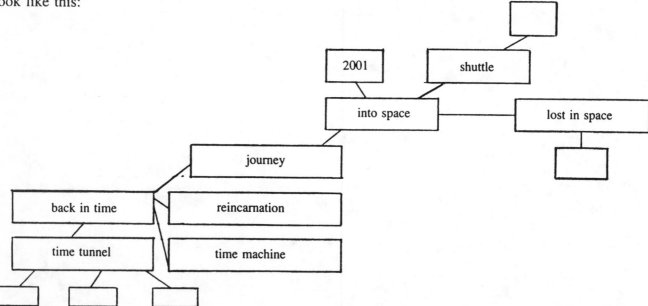

Notice that the strings connect related ideas. A new branch means a new idea. A cluster may have as few as three branches or as many as six or seven when completed.

When all have added a card, have each student then write a related *detail* and connect to any one of the subtopics. Several cards may describe what the time tunnel looks like, while "Discovery" may name the "shuttle" and a possible destination could connect to "lost in space."

Processing Out

Discuss the value of the free flow of ideas as a pre-writing activity. Discuss any comments students have about the process of developing the cluster. Ask:

—Would anyone like to change any cards? (This often happens. Students analyze relationships of ideas and feel there's a ''better'' place for something. Stay out of the way—let the group decide. You may need more cards!)

Follow-up Activity

Divide the class into groups, one for each branch and ask them to develop that idea into a short story or essay.

—Individually, cluster ''journey'' (or another word) on paper and write a short vignette afterward. When clustering on paper, suggest that they continue to trace over boxes and lines while thinking so the pencil continues to move at all times. The clustering should continue until the student allows enough time to exhaust many ideas and ''feels'' a sense of the direction that the vignette will take. Many ideas in the cluster may never be used in the actual writing, but it is important to take the time to list them.

-NOTES-

(10) WRITING GUIDED FANTASIES

Purpose

To introduce a simple formula for writing guided fantasies.

Preparation

(Be sure that students have already been exposed to the guided fantasy. It would be difficult to write a guided fantasy, otherwise. I would suggest the ones included in the Introductory Imagery Activity section, those found in my first book, *200 Ways of Using Imagery in the Classroom* or Beverly Galyean's *Mind Sight*.)

First ask students to make a list of at least 10 places they'd like to visit right now. These may be places they have or have not actually visited. When finished, have them skim the list and select the one that really stands out as being the most important to them at this time. Have them rewrite the name of that place in the center of a new page, circle it, and use either the clustering or multi-sensory clustering technique to get ideas about it. When finished, ask them to put their pens down and close their eyes.

Image

Go to the place right now...see yourself there...notice how you're dressed...and how good it feels to be here...scan the entire scene, taking in every detail...(longer pause)...notice sounds...smells...and tastes...when you've gotten a vivid mental picture of the place, open your eyes, pick up your pen and add to your cluster if you'd like to. Then recreate this place for others by writing a guided fantasy. Follow the rules listed (on the board).

Write

Rules for Writing a Guided Fantasy
—Write 10 to 12 lines
—Begin each line with a verb (i.e., see, notice, listen, etc.)
—Make statements—don't ask questions (i.e., "See the colors" not "Do you see the colors?")
—Try to include all of the senses.
—Begin with statements that are general, to establish where you are (i.e., "See yourself at the circus, park, beach," etc.) and go to specifics ("smell the popcorn,")
—Keep statements focussed on positive feelings and safe actions. (Avoid going underground, under water or in the air.)
—End with a line such as, "Feel yourself returning to the classroom" or "Bring your awareness back to this room."

Follow-up Activity

—Have students proofread each other's guided fantasies, checking to see if the guidelines have been followed.

—After proofreading, share some of these with the class and have them write about the experience.

—Share the guided fantasy below which is a good example of a visit to a place that does not exist. Then have students try writing one like it.

A VISIT TO THE LAND OF BLUE
By Marion H. McLaughlin

Image

See yourself in the Land of Blue
See the brilliant blue sky
Notice the white clouds against the blue sky
See the birds flying near them
See yourself walking along the ocean blue
Look down into the blue water
See your blue image
Smile
Notice the life under the surface
Hear the roar of a motorboat
Smell the fish
Leave the beach and walk to a park
See the field of blue on our flag
Spot a bird's nest with three light blue eggs in it
See a parade of all blue objects
Decorate your room in shades of blue
Review all you've seen in the Land of Blue
Slowly return to our classroom
When I count to ten open your eyes

THE SOUND OF A POET

Most people think I write poems
about other people,
But not so.
I don't always write to make
    a point,
...or send my love.
I don't always write to show
    people my inner soul—
I write to myself, to show me
    my inner soul;
To listen to my heart sound.
I sing to me to cheer my mind
And for the catharsis which
I could never let out, for fear
Of hurting someone (like myself).
"Escape" is the road I travel
Where I can be free to fly
    or drown,
Where I don't have to be better
    than anyone but me...

Kathleen Brennan, Grade 12

CHAPTER SIX

Poetry

Warm-Ups

MY TENSION IS GONE!

Most students have a great deal of fear when asked to write poetry. This activity is a symbolic one. Tell them to imagine that they are collecting all of the tension that exists in their bodies. "Feel it rising from your feet and legs...feel it draining down from your neck, head and shoulders...pull all of the tension together and imagine that it is now traveling down your arm to your pen...force all of that tension into your pen...and now write, 'MY TENSION IS GONE!' Wad up the paper and throw it away. Your tension is indeed gone and all writing will be easy."

DRAMATIZATION OF POETRY

Getting over the fear of the unknown (poetry) is easy with this activity. I like to use the poetry of Shel Silverstein for this since it is outrageously funny and nonthreatening. Divide the class into groups and give each a copy of a different poem. Tell them that they must "present" the poem to the rest of the class in an interesting way. They may act it out, put it to music, recite it in a novel way, etc. All students must take an active part—speaking or acting. Encourage them to cut apart the copy so each may memorize his lines. Allow one class period for planning and practice. Present poems the following day. Follow-up with student-selected poetry and more serious themes later.

CONVERTING PROSE

Demonstrate that prose is not really that different from poetry. Begin with a paragraph from a story or newspaper article and instruct students to strike out unnecessary words from each sentence. Then rewrite the passage as a poem, retaining the original meaning. Each line could contain from one word to one phrase—students should make that determination based upon the emphasis they wish to give, (one word on a line calls greater attention to it). It is especially interesting to use the same passage with all students and then compare the results. This activity also reinforces MAIN IDEA.

GROUP POEM

Sculpture, artwork, objects in nature or slides and pictures from your picture file can be the motivational stimulus for a group poem. Each member should write his strongest impression on a 3x5 card after viewing the motivational item. Next ask the group to share what is on the cards and rearrange them to form the lines of a poem. Additions and rewriting are acceptable.

CONCRETE POETRY

CONCRETE POETRY is the use of words and their physical formation to convey meaning. This may be done with color, the shape of the letters, and/or the arrangement of words. Samples below show some of the many variations possible.

Purpose

To call attention to the concrete idea that the words represent. To encourage use of evocative language.

Materials

Pens/markers and paper.

Procedure

Ask students to graphically create a scene using only words. From a distance this will look like a picture but up close, it will consist only of words and phrases. No extra lines or shapes should be used. You may wish to suggest that a light pencil line be drawn first as a guide. Encourage the use of colors, shapes and sizes that will enhance the meaning of words.

SAMPLES

Using single words to convey meaning.

Concrete Poetry by Alice Trachtenbroit

Using words to describe an object, creating the shape of the object by "filling" it with those words.

Concrete Poetry by Wendy Dembeck

Concrete Poetry by Susan Blank

```
                 W
                ith
              golden
              sparks
               and
                y
            ellowwhit
            eradiance
            Ilightthe
            wayforall
            tosee.Bor
            nofathous
            anddrippi
            ngsintoac
            auldronof
            moltenpar
            rafinmyst
            urdystalk
            proudlypr
            oclaimsmy
            usefulnes
            s.Ishine,
            flicker,i
            lluminate,
            causingcat
            eyestogleam
            ,champagn e!
            !tosparkl  e,
            roomstobe  com
            ecozyandi  nti
            mateaslov  ers
            'smilesgl  ow
            .Ibrighte  n,
          andcomfort.Iamc
          andle.Iamlight.
```

Using words to describe the parts of objects in a scene.

Concrete Poetry by
Robert Shapiro

IMAGES

IMAGES are short formula poems used to evoke mental pictures. They make use of language that appeals to the senses; are clear, precise and direct.

Purpose

To try many variations of the same basic formula in order to create an awareness of the limitlessness of language.

Materials

Picture File

Procedure

Have students select pictures which are not "busy," (having only one or two subjects in them). Since these are "real subjects, the first time around, students will be merely describing what is in the picture. Each time the basic formula is to be followed, but the imagery directions will begin to change what is in the picture. After all of the options have been presented, students can experiment on their own with new subjects.

Follow the sequence below:

Write

Study the picture you have chosen and then write a description using the following formula:
LINE #1: Describe the object with two or three adjectives
LINE #2: Give the object action
LINE #3: Put the object somewhere

SHARE WHAT HAS BEEN WRITTEN AFTER EACH SET OF DIRECTIONS.

Image

Close your eyes and see the object in the picture...the color...shape...size...now see the object doing something really silly...or someone doing something really silly with it...open your eyes and use the same formula to write about this. Title it, "Real & Silly."

Image

Close your eyes again and see the object...this time make something strange happen to it or with it...notice where this is happening...open your eyes and write. Title it, "Real and Strange."

Image

Close your eyes again and see this object in a sad way...notice where it is happening...feel the sadness...open your eyes and write. Title it, "Real & Sad."

Write & Image

Continue to make changes in any way you wish in order to write images for the following titles:
"Real & Beautiful"
"Unreal & Beautiful"
"Unreal & Strange"
"Unreal & Silly"
"Unreal & Sad"

SHARE WHAT HAS BEEN WRITTEN, LETTING STUDENTS GUESS THE TITLE/CATEGORY OF EACH OTHER'S IMAGES.

Follow-up

Create characters that fall into the different categories. Image objects having human qualities (personification). Create images for characters and settings of stories read in class. Use alliteration, similes and metaphors.

SAMPLES

Ice cream cone
pastel pink wrapped in a tan blanket
painting a picture
on a little boy's face.
    Gail A. Katz, Gr. 9

A winged snake
hissing
in the sea
poking out and flying upward.
    Pietro Michelucci, Gr. 9

A wild white stallion
holding his head high and tail outstreched
his long white mane
flowing in the wind as he gallops
down a deserted beach at the hour of dawn
possessing spirit
independence
and pride.
    Tom Gilmore, Gr. 11

A jewel-adorned hummingbird
just bathed in scented oil
lavishing on the tingling sweet
nectar of a honeysuckle, blooming
in a crystal meadow of sunlight.
    Deborah Harwood, Gr. 10

An ugly frowning pumpkin
singing eerie Halloween songs,
in the dead of night.
    Patricia Tironi, Gr. 11

A single blade of grass
green, crisp and young
protruding through the blanket
of white crystalline snow
waiting patiently for Spring
to sweep over the earth.
    Kim Miller, Gr. 10

EMOTION POETRY

EMOTION POETRY is short lyric poetry describing an emotion in terms of the action or events surrounding it. Rhyme is not necessary.

Purpose

To evoke emotions in the reader with vivid descriptions of a scene.

Preparation

Brainstorm with students to get a long list of emotions on the board. Generate as many words as is possible, using synonyms, (fear and afraid) too. Then ask students to select one of the words and write it at the top of their papers followed by the word 'is.' (i.e., Anger is...)

Image

Close your eyes now and look out of a window to see a scene that reflects that emotion...notice who it is that is feeling that emotion...notice what is happening in the scene...every little detail...open your eyes when you feel that you have gotten a clear picture, and describe that emotion in terms of what was happening in the scene.

Follow-up

Select another word and repeat. Draw an illustration or find a picture to go with the poem.

SAMPLES

Happy is
Running, jumping, smiling
Falling down from too much laughter
Happy
    Laura A. Gebhart, Gr. 11

Hostility is
A snarling boy,
A fierce lion with mouth open wide,
Devouring a meek child.
    Kris DiPalma, Gr. 7

Frustration is
Playing tag
And never catching anyone
    Carolyn Grau, Gr. 9

Loneliness is
A faceless being
Standing on a high cliff
Waves raging below
Smothered by darkness.
    Tom Klein, Gr. 9

HAIKU

HAIKU POETRY is a form of Japanese poetry which had its origins in HOKKU, an older form. Although most English texts insist on a rigid form of three lines containing seventeen syllables, (5-7-5), this is really a western adaptation based on mistranslation of the Japanese. (I never burden students with this 5-7-5 rule, but rather ask them to focus on the here-and-now concepts being written about.) Usually HAIKU uses nature as its focus, but American poets have written on other topics that link nature to human nature. Rhyme is not necessary.

Purpose

To introduce Haiku poetry to students.

Materials

Each student should have 3 blank 3x5 cards. Use nature pictures if it is not possible to go outside or look at nature through a window.

Procedure

Either take students on a short walk together, ask them to observe on their own (after school, at home) or take a few minutes of class time to look out the window and observe something in nature. Suggest that they find one object to 'zero in on.' Do not discuss the observations. They may jot down some notes as they observe.

Write

When ample time has been given, (don't rush it) instruct them to write the following on each of the cards: (1) a phrase describing the object observed—may include adjectives, alliteration (2) a phrase or series of words describing the action of the object—may include verbs and adverbs (3) something significant about the object—a tiny detail about it, the thoughts of the object, where it is at the moment, how it does or does not fit into the 'bigger picture,' etc.

When the cards are done, (give directions one card at a time) have students place the cards on the desk and rearrange them until there is a flow and rhythm to the three lines when read in succession. Some modifications may be necessary to create this flow. When satisfied, recopy the poem's three lines as one poem.

Follow-up

Illustrate the Haiku. Write it using calligraphy. Describe events at school in this way.

SAMPLES:

Withered leaf clinging
Dry, brittle, but tenacious
On the tree of life.
    Mary E. Evansburg

Ancient rock cliffs
Silently lose themselves to the sea
Forever.
    Karin K. Hess

SUGGESTED RESOURCES FOR TEACHING HAIKU

Atwood, A. *Haiku: The Mood of the Earth*. N.Y.: Charles Scribner's Sons, 1971.
Literature for Children (filmstrip series that includes haiku, legends, fables, etc.) Pied Piper, P.O. Box 320, Verdugo City, CA 91046.

CONTRAST POETRY

CONTRAST POETRY depicts the same object, person or idea in two different ways, beginning with the most obvious association and moving to, perhaps, an unusual or strikingly different vantage point. Rhyming couplets may be used but rhyme is not necessary.

Purpose

To use the power of evocative language to create and then recreate an image of the same thing, person or idea.

Materials

Word Cards or pictures from your Picture File.

Preparation

Have students select a picture or word card before you begin. If pictures are used, provide extra time to become familiar with them and ask students to then choose only one object in the picture to focus upon. Once decided, that word which describes the object or the word from the card, becomes the title of the poem.

Image

Close your eyes and see the object in your mind's eye...scan the scene to see where the object is...notice sounds...smells...textures...of this place...feel the mood of this scene...examine the object once more...watch as it begins to change...very slightly...remaining the same, yet becoming maybe stronger or older or younger...watch the qualities that remain the same...see the ones that are now drastically different...examine the new scene...observe the mood...and any details...remember how the object used to be...change it back to the way it was...when I count to 5, bring your awareness back to the room and prepare to begin writing.

Write

Use the following formula to show the contrast:

TITLE: Name of object or person

LINE #1-#2 or #3: Write two or three lines that paint a vivid picture of the initial image.

SKIP A LINE

LINES #4-#5 or #6: Write two or three lines that paint a different picture. Try also to follow whatever pattern your first lines took.(i.e., If Line #2 contains two adjectives and a noun, then so should Line #4.)

Follow-up

Try Contrast Poems for showing changes in story characters, traditions, environment, etc.

OUTRAGEOUS THEMES

FANTASY is based upon whimsical or surreal images, imagination images. It takes the familiar and makes it strange or takes the strange and has it become familiar.

Purpose

To encourage creative thinking and new directions for 'ordinary' occurrences. To incorporate humor into writing.

Preparation

I usually set the mood for this writing by reading some of the poetry of Shel Silverstein. Because he uses rhyme, I also suggest that students try to write using rhyme. I use animals as the theme for this activity but any topic will work.

Have students choose an animal to write about before you begin.

Image
Close your eyes and see the animal that you have chosen...notice its color...shape...size...watch it move...see it doing something that is typical for that animal to do...now make a change in the animal...change it in a ridiculous way...experiment with changing the color...size...body features...now see the animal in the most outrageous way that you'd like...see how this will effect the way it does something...when you think that you have gotten an idea to write about, open your eyes and begin.

Write

First jot down any ideas that you got during the imagery. These may be words or phrases. Next to some/any of the words, add a rhyming word or two. When you have a paper full of ideas, try to describe the animal in a humorous way, using rhyme. (You may wish to use one of the formulas in later activities.)

Follow-up

Illustrate your poem. Select other themes to write about.

Sample

The poem and illustration below were done by Laura A. Gebhart, Grade 11.

The Dachshund Giraffe

His neck is as high as an escalator
His body is just as long
But his legs are short and stubby
And his movements are all wrong.

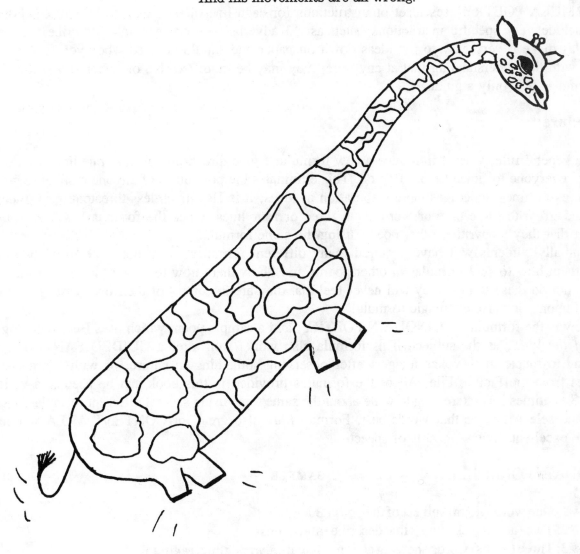

FORMULA POETRY

FORMULA POETRY uses a set of instructions for each line of the poem to be written. Formulas may include very specific instructions, such as, '3 adverbs' or very general, 'describe the action.' Formulas make it very easy to put ideas down on paper and should be used when you first introduce poetry with the understanding that at any time, they may be modified. No one should feel locked into the formula. It is only a guide.

Procedure

As a general rule, when I introduce a new formula, I give directions for only one line at a time and wait for everyone to finish before I go on. This eliminates the possibility of anyone rushing to get done and the extra time encourages more elaboration of ideas. It is also much less threatening to students to be asked to write three or four words than three or four lines. Once the formula has been shared, I suggest that they try writing other poems using the same formula.

Eventually students will have acquired many different formulas. It is then time to do two things: Show them how to find formulas in other poems and Show them how to create their own formulas. If you do not do these things, they will never feel that they are in control of their own writing, but rather depend upon you for the "magic formula!"

Below is the formula for CINQUAIN POETRY, and a sample poem which uses Buck, the dog from *Call of the Wild*, as the subject. This formula also works well after a GUIDED FANTASY, while listening to music that evokes images, after observing something in nature, or with Word Cards or pictures from the Picture File. All of the formulas provided in this book can be used in a variety of ways. Sometimes it is interesting to write about the same topic using several different formulas, compare them and select the one that words best. Formulas are also great for CONTENT AREA writing and provide excellent review of parts of speech!

CINQUAIN FORMULA: SAMPLE:

LINE #1: One word/(noun) subject of the poem Buck—
LINE #2: Two (adjectives) words that describe Alert, Tense;
LINE #3: Three (verbs) words showing action Snarling, wrangling, raging
LINE #4: Four words relating to a feeling Earning life through battle,
LINE #5: One word that repeats or refers to Wolf.
       the subject in line #1.
                                        by Margaret Giles

You need not look further than your classroom for formulas. Have students divide into groups and devise some of their own *with a sample poem to go with it*. The sample is important because it proves that the formula works. Some groups will begin with a formula and then try to write a sample; others will begin with a topic and vacillate between sample and formula; still others will write a poem and then figure out what the formula is! There is no right or wrong way. Let them go and you will be surprised with what they come up with.

Below are some formulas with sample poems which were written by groups of teachers taking my Creative Writing course. Remember...modify the formula if it doesn't work for you!

FORMULAS	SAMPLES
#1: participle, participle, participle	Leaping, soaring, flying
#2: noun	The superhero
#3: adverb (how)	Nonchalantly
#4: verb	Crashed
#5: where or when	Into the wall.
Title: Pick a color	Green
#1: describe something associated with it	Makes me think of Spring
#2: simile/metaphor	Like a tree covered with leaves
#3: where	in a wooded forest.
Title: Pick a color*	Blue
#1: color + noun	Blue sky
#2: verb + color	Running blue
#3: adverb + color	Cloudy blue
#4: superlative	Bluest!

*The above formula also works if you substitute an *adjective* for the color.

#1: a place	School
#2: sounds heard there	Crashing lockers
#3: when	Before homeroom
#4: describe some action	Scurrying to beat the bell
#5: describe mood	Worried about a test.
Title: emotion	Jealousy
#1: two or three colors associated with it	Green, yellow, black
#2: It happens when	It happens when I can't have it.
#3: I feel like	I feel like a snake hiding
	in the grass
#4: three sensory words	Hissing, lurking, malicious.
Title: feeling	Silly
#1: three verbs	Tickle, wiggle, giggle
#2: where	Lying on the floor
#3: who has the feeling	My baby sister.
Title: noun	Giraffes
#1: verb	Munching
#2: verb phrase	Loping in the grass
#3: three adjectives	Stately, long-necked, silent.

Title: participle	Jumping
#1: three nouns that do it	Frogs, kangaroos, Mexican beans
#2: two adjectives (how)	Happy, playful
#3: simile	Like a singing heart.

Title: Earliest Memory	Earliest Memory
#1: Where	At the easel
#2: doing what	Painting a sailboat
#3: two or three words that show emotion	Intense, quiet, relaxed
#4: detail from the setting	Too much water on the brush
#5: skip a line	
#6: tell how you feel	Frustrated.

PAPA VINC	Wow!
Can your students	Clouds
guess what the eight	are floating
letters of PAPA VINC	across the blue sky
stand for?	anxiously reminding
Write eight lines, beginning	all of us
each one with a different	to smile
part of speech.	by Joe Mastropolo

NOTE: These formulas can be adapted to prose writing very easily in any of the following ways:

(1) First write a poem using the formula, then write a short story, each poem line being the main idea of each paragraph in the story. This encourages elaboration.

(2) Use the formula to determine how each sentence in a paragraph will begin. This encourages variety of sentence structure.

(3) Since most expository writing also follows a formula, have students try using those to write poetry. (See formulas below)

Feature Story Formula

Headline   (Title)
By-line   (Author)
Lead   (First paragraph/main idea/captures interest)
Body   (Gives facts not in Lead/short, well-organized paragraphs)
Conclusion   (May refer back to Lead/Ties up loose ends)

Essay Formula

Introduction   (States opinion/Goes from broad statement to specific point)
Body   (Reasons for opinion/does away with objections/saves best for last)
Conclusion   (Restates opinion/makes broad, general statement)

Argument Formula

Similar to ESSAY, may be one or several paragraphs
Introduction   (States opinion/Broad statement)
Body   (Reasons/facts/examples)
Conclusion   (Sums up argument)

NOTE: Pictures and word cards are great for sparking themes for expository writing.

MODELING

MODELING means using a poem that has been written as the formula for other poems. Teachers who must teach a unit on poetry will find this useful, taking the poems to be covered in class, and having students write a poem which parallels the one being studied.

Three poems and three different approaches are included in this section. I encourage you to adapt any or all of these ideas to your study of poetry. Students who learn by modeling usually have much better retention of the poems covered.

Purpose

To introduce poetry and poetic style.

Fog
by Carl Sandburg

Preparation

Read the poem, *Fog*, together in class. Discuss mood, personification, etc. as you normally would. Brainstorm, (listing at the board) other forces of nature besides fog, (i.e. snow, sleet, etc.), asking students to then select one that they wish to write about.

Image

Close your eyes and see the force of nature that you have chosen to write about...observe it in its very gentlest form...watch now as its strength begins to build...becoming more and more forceful...almost violent...see how it moves and what it does...now watch as this force becomes an animal...notice the animal's color...size and movements...observe the animal in its most powerful state...watch now as the animal becomes gentle...and quiet...see the way it now moves...and where it is...change the animal back into the original force of nature...and watch as it drifts away from that place...when I count to five, open your eyes.

Write

You will now write about that force of nature using the formula below. You will notice that it is similar to the way *Fog* is written.

    TITLE: Nature Form chosen
    LINE #1: Title + (how it arrives or begins/as the animal would arrive)
    LINE #2: Tell what it does
    LINE #3: and how it does it
    LINE #4: and where it is
    LINE #5: Tell how it leaves/as the animal would leave
    LINES #2-4 may be interchanged for a better flow of the language.

SAMPLES

Mist

Mist arrives quietly,
softly,
breezily
like a hawk in flight
It glides, swiftly,
hovering below the treetops,
above the ground.
Then, silently, peacefully,
soars away.
Debbie Glaser, Gr. 7

Lightning

The lightning glides in
with its tremendous wings.
It covers the sky with
its flashes and glides
as it looks over the entire world
with its great eyes of fire.
It leaves slowly and silently
as it brightens the sky
with its wings of color.
Robin May, Gr. 7

Lightning

Raging, terrifying lightning
comes in a thrashing wolf attacking.
Vicious streaks
leap in and out of nowhere
as they tear
at the countryside below.
Christina Bonner, Gr. 7

Wind

The wind dances in on
trotting horses feet
It stops in a golden
Valley looking about through
Fiery eyes, and then rages past
at a mighty gallop.
Jenny Kurnath, Gr. 7

Wind

the wind comes in as free as a bird
quietly riding over the mountains
unaware of what it's doing
coming and going whenever it pleases.
Donna Varga, Gr. 7

Is My Team Ploughing
by A. E. Houseman

Preparation

This idea comes from English teacher, Dorothy Ramundo. She wrote a guided fantasy and read that to the class before they read *Is My Team Ploughing?*

Image

Relax. Let your imagination drift off...
See yourself in a life beyond this one...
See yourself as having left this world...
Think that you died, but you are curious about how things are going without you...
Let this curiosity cause you to worry a bit about some of your earthly dreams...
Imagine that you are able to ask an old friend four questions...
Hope that the answers you hear will make you feel better...
Begin to think about your earthly life...
Think maybe about how life might not be as good for others now that you are gone...
Ask your friend a question about your work...
Hear him answer in a surprising way...
Ask your friend about sports and fun that you had together...
Hear him answer in a surprising way...
Let your curiosity go a bit beyond...
Ask your friend about your girl and how she's surviving without you...
Hear him give an answer that is surprising...
Ask your friend about himself...
Hear an answer that shocks you!...
Ask yourself what it all means...
Come back to reality. At the count of five, open your eyes...1...2...3...4...5.

Write

After the guided fantasy, have students write eight stanzas, each one either beginning with a question they might ask a good friend after they are dead or with his reply. Suggest to them that they should try to show some irony in the last answer given.

Follow-up

Share the ballads written by students and then read *Is My Team Ploughing?* and compare it to what students wrote.

SAMPLES

How is my store,
        down on Broadway and Leigh?
Sales have gone down,
        I'm sure without me.

No, not at all,
        Business is booming.
With all the new customers,
        Cash flow is zooming.

The team must be losing,
        I'm certain of that.
Bob can't throw a ball,
        Jim can't swing a bat.

As a matter of fact,
        They're 16 and 0.
We're the new state champs,
        Didn't you know?

How is my girlfriend,
        Is she pulling through?
Will she survive?
        What will she do?

Don't fret about Jane;
        Don't be misled.
On next Sunday
        She will be wed.

What about you?
        Although I am gone,
Your loyalty to me
        Will still linger on.

Enough of these questions!
        You're out of the way.
Now Jane and I can prepare
        For our wedding day.
                Sharon Saunders, Gr. 10

How are things at work?
Who took my job?
Is the new boss good,
        or is he a snob?

We got some young guy
His name is Jake.
He even lets us drink beers
on our coffee break.

How's the team doing?
Are we still in third place,
or after I died
did the team fall on its face?

We got a new pitcher.
His name is Chip.
He pitched the rest of the season.,
We won the championship.

How is Allyson?
Is she O.K.?
Or does she stay home
and cry every day?

She looks fine.
She seems to be alright.
I see her with a new guy
each and every night

How about you, Joe?
How did you feel when you heard I was dead?
Did it really hurt you
or just confuse your head?

It didn't really hurt me,
I really felt O.K.
because I never liked
anything about you anyway.
                Ed Kelly, Gr. 10

How's the business going?
Are we still in debt?
No, we've made so much money
I bought a Corvette

Is our softball team still losing?
Are we still in last place?
No, we've made a complete turnaround.
We're in the heat of the pennant race

Is my girlfriend surviving without me?
Is she still very weak?
No, she's one of the happiest people around,
because she's getting married next week.

Do you ever plan on settling down
and finding yourself a wife
Yes, I'm marrying your ex-girlfriend.
We're going to have a great life!

    Jamie Pestone, Gr. 10

What If. . .
by Steve Vazquez

Preparation

Read the poem, *What If...?* together with the class. Notice that many lines begin with the last thought of the previous line. Using this as a guide for writing, tell students to write the first line, beginning with the words, *What if* and completing it with any thoughts that they have. Line #2 should then use part of #1 in its question, and so on. End with *What if...?* Encourage themes and ideas that are universal and important to mankind and the world.

Image

(Students should feel free to stop at the end of each line and image on their own for ideas. I suggest playing soft music during the actual writing time.)

WHAT IF...?
What if love was ever present and all we had to do was open our eyes to see it?
What if fear was just an illusion, a created delusion like the figures we fantasize in a shadow?
What if your fantasies were real and life was actually a dream?
What if death was really a doorway to life and a reminder to live each moment?
What if each moment of sadness was really only a way our hearts beacon us to make a change in our lifes?
What if life was only a humorous story?
What if laughter was the golden key to the cosmos?
What if the cosmos was really one giant thought?
What if thought was only a mechanism to bring joy?
What if joy increased each time it was given away?
What if we gave away trust to strangers and saw each old relationship with new freshness of a new encounter?
What if each violent encounter was greeted with kindness and kindness greeted with thankfulness?
What if thankfulness brought automatic understanding?
What if understanding was seen as beauty?
What if beauty was a commonplace thing that we see in each puddle, each word and each person?
What if each person and thing they do was a gift designed to bring each of us a special learning?
What if each learning helped connect us to other people?
What if other people were really a part of ourselves like a toe is part of the foot?
What if feet were handled as carefully as faces?
What if faces were really only vehicles for beaming warmth and light?
What if warmth and light were the basics from which all things were built?
What if all things built were constructed for their harmony with nature?
What if nature's plants and animals were revered like humans?
What if humans spent as much time and money on peace as differences?
What if differences were celebrated as uniqueness?
What if uniquesness was as precious as gold?
What if gold shone only when one smiled?
What if smiling brought good health automatically?
What if things are really what you want them to be and accepting "what is" is the way to be free?
What if...?

BALLADS

BALLADS are a type of narrative poetry that tell a story. Often they are put to music and contain a refrain that is repeated throughout. Ballads, originally passed down from generation to generation by being sung, contained themes that were emotional—sad, happy, romantic, heroic or humorous.

Purpose

To introduce the BALLAD and then write one, either in small groups of individually.

Procedure

I like to introduce the ballad with songs by such artists as Harry Chapin, Neil Diamond, Paul Simon or Kris Kristofferson. Afterwards, students will begin to suggest other music that fits the definition of a ballad and will feel comfortable with it. (They will also become aware that all music began with a poet *and* a musician, not just the latter.) From this point, I offer three different approaches to writing ballads.

ACTIVITY#1

Begin with an instrumental piece of music. This can be a professional recording or better yet, an original song by one of your students. (Ask your school music teacher for a list of students who have the talent to write music. This is an excellent way to validate that student's talent!) Play the recording several times for your class, asking them to merely listen the first time and later, to jot down notes about the impressions they are getting from the music. During the next class session, while the music is again being played softly, suggest that they put their notes together as phrases and then rearrange the phrases in such an order that they follow a story line. On the third day, have students pay close attention to the music's rhythm as they silently read their phrases, making adjustments by rearranging words or changing them. Encourage them to state their basic theme in the refrain.

Please note that this activity will take several class sessions and numerous playings of the recording are imperative. The tune must play in the students' own heads for them to write meaningful lyrics. Allow time for the creative process; it's well worth the time spent!

ACTIVITY #2

Begin with a guided fantasy, asking the class to "go to their workshops," (After inspecting it and getting comfortable there, sit down in a chair in front of the viewing screen.) Now begin any guided fantasy, making the suggestion that they are gathering ideas for the writing of a ballad, and should make mental notes along the way. When you have finished, ask students to begin to write the story in such a way that it could be sung as a ballad. Later they may wish to put it to music.

You may want to divide the class into groups for the actual writing for this activity. Group them according to the themes they wish to focus on. The individual ideas will given energy to the central theme.

ACTIVITY #3

Begin with the CHARACTER DEVELOPMENT student page found in the Appendix. Create a character's history before doing the imagery below since the imagery will take the character through a sequence of events. Students may wish to use a name from the phone book, an historical figure, a character from a story or a picture to get started. Once completed, begin the imagery.

Image

See the character that you have created as he or she would look if sleeping...notice the face...and each feature of it...it is early morning...and your character is just waking up...notice the surroundings...watch the character stretch, and go through whatever routine would be typical for the character...see a typical day for that character...paying attention to where the character goes...what the character does and whom the character does it with...the day is coming to an end...as the character begins to drift off to sleep, read his or her thoughts about a past memory...read the character's thoughts about a future dream or desire...as I count to ten, bring your awareness back to the room...1...2...3...4...5...6...7...8...9...10.

Write

Write your story about this character in the form of a ballad. You may wish to use one of the formulas to get you started. Make sure that the refrain contains the central theme.

SAMPLE

Here is a ballad written by Elaine Ball, Grade 12.

She sits at home and watches soaps;
She knows the feeling well.
She feels so empty and alone;
The white walls form her cell.

She gazes at the T.V. set;
She's in her daily trance.
She waits for someone to come home
Although there is no chance.

She shuts her eyes and wishes hard;
She needs a voice's sound.
She opens them and looks about;
Her heart drops to the ground.

She doesn't want to leave the house;
She doesn't want to stay.
She doesn't have a place to go
And cannot get away.

She has no friends to comfort her;
She has no where to turn.
She cannot deal with people
And is petrified to learn.

She sits at home and watches soaps;
She knows the feeling well.
She feels so empty and alone
And can't escape her cell.

Tell me. . .
I forget.

Show me. . .
I remember.

Involve me. . .
I understand.
Ancient Chinese Proverb

CHAPTER SEVEN

Drama

WARM-UPS

VOCABULARY CHARADES

As an alternative way to introduce new vocabulary words, assign one new word to each student in the class. For homework, the students must look up the word and devise a way to act out the meaning. Members of the class may ask *yes-no* questions (I usually set a limit to how many) to clarify meanings. If the words come from a text, students should use that meaning/situation as the basis of the charade.

ONE MINUTE ON STAGE

Since students often fear getting up in front of the class, take time to make each one stand in front of the group for a full minute. Suggest that the time will go more quickly if they are *doing* something—anything! (Reading, telling jokes, counting ceiling blocks, etc.) Challenge them to be creative with their minute.

RECORD PANTOMINES

Groups of students can select a favorite song to lip sync. Successful presentations should be based on body language interpretations of the music, group unity and synchronization of lips to the lyrics.

OBJECT CHARADES

On cards write the names of household machines and ask each student to select one. Each should then come to the front of the room and act out *being* the object (*not* using it). Suggest that they not make any sounds while showing how the object works. The class can guess what the appliance is. This can also be done in pairs. (Variation: Student holding the card gives directions to another, who does not know what he is demonstrating).

SIGN A SONG (OR POEM, STORY, ETC.)

Have students interpret a song's words, using sign language. If resources are not available to learn signing, students should create their own sign language.

CREATING A TABLEAU

A TABLEAU is a static depiction of a scene, usually presented on a stage by costumed actors.

Purpose

To use passive drama to convey meaning to an audience.

Procedure

Creating tableaux is great for the students who feel uncomfortable acting, because all they have to do is strike a pose. You may wish to begin with a famous painting, such as *Washington Crossing the Delaware* and simply ask students to take the pose of each of the people in the painting. This will give them the feel for what a tableau is. Then do any of the following activities below:

ACTIVITY #1

If you use a painting or picture for the students to recreate, try having them image the thoughts of the people they are pretending to be. Then when they create the tableau, each can, one at a time, relax his pose and speak his thoughts to the audience without being heard by the others, who are still frozen in the moment.

Image

Before you create the tableau, you will see yourself becoming the character you have chosen to be. Close your eyes...and see yourself as the person in the painting...notice how you are dressed...feel the texture of the cloth...and how it feels against your skin...look around and see the others in the picture...notice the expression on each person's face...try to read their thoughts...now focus on your own thoughts...think about the circumstances that have brought you to this place and time...think of your loved ones somewhere...and how they are feeling right now...look to the future...of things to come after this moment...and what those things will mean to you...speak your thoughts to yourself...and notice what you are feeling...slowly bring your awareness back to this room...when I count to ten, begin to write the thoughts that you had as the character in the picture...1...2...3...4...5...6...7...8...9...10.

Write & Act

First write your monologue, noting voice tone, inflections, hand gestures, etc. so that you can recite it later as part of the tableau.

ACTIVITY #2

Begin with cards with vocabulary words on them (I like to start with adjectives and progress from there). Instruct students to first image a pose that would demonstrate the meaning of the word, (i.e. grotesque). One by one, call on them to come to the front of the room take that pose and hold it, making sure that they are touching at least one of the other students when they join the tableau. Eventually you will have a scene that epitomizes your word. It will also serve as a means of finding out if the students actually do understand the meaning of the word. Question the remaining students as to what the vocabulary word means and make adjustments if they are needed. Students will remember the tableau when studying the vocabulary words because they now take on a personal meaning for them.

ACTIVITY #3

Group students and give them time to create their own tableaux for the rest of the class. They may wish to select a scene from a short story or play, event in history or incorporate several vocabulary words together to form a meaningful scene. Each should image the scene as the character he will portray and then work it into the bigger picture.

IMAGING ACTION

IMAGING ACTION of characters before acting it out helps actors see the subtle activities that will make a character more believable. The imagery sets up the scene and allows the character to do whatever would be typical, given the circumstances.

Purpose

To develop believable actions and reactions before performing a role.

Preparation

Discuss with students what they might be doing at a bus stop while waiting for a bus on a very cold day. (Typical responses are: jumping up and down, rubbing hands together, blowing on hands, shivering, etc.) Tell them that they are going to image being at that bus stop to see what they might do. Later discuss and compare the actions of waiting at a bus stop for a bus on a very cold day.

Image

Close your eyes...see yourself at a bus stop in the middle of winter...notice how you are dressed...from your head...to your feet...feel the coldness of the air...see your breath as you exhale...pull your clothing around you more tightly...look up at the sign that says bus stop...look into the streets for the bus that is already 10 minutes late...observe your surroundings...and any other people...feel a sharp, cold gust of wind blow up under your coat...try to do something about the cold...find some way to relieve your miserable condition...feel yourself warming up...as you bring yourself back to the classroom...when I count to ten open your eyes.

Follow-Up

Discuss any differences between the answers that were brainstormed and those that were imaged. Pantomime what was imaged. Write guided fantasies that set up other circumstances to be acted out. Use plays to be performed or studied to determine actions and stage directions for them. Write original acts to plays by alternating imaging and writing to gain new ideas for dialogue and actions.

MASTERY REHEARSAL

MASTERY REHEARSAL is the mental practicing of a performance or presentation in a positive way, so as to minimize nervousness.

Purpose

To prepare for an oral presentation.

Preparation

(Although this activity is written for an oral presentation it can be adapted to any type of performance. Teachers who have taken my courses have written imageries for performing scenes of a play, preparing for what they will do in case a prop is missing or a cue is missed, singing or dancing on stage, accepting an award, etc. The applications are endless.)

The imaging is to be done after students have researched a topic, taken notes, developed an outline and written out their presentations on cards. I usually do this the day before the oral presentation is due and make the suggestion that they repeat it before they go to sleep that night, as opposed to going to sleep worrying about how they will do.

Image

See yourself standing up in front of the room ready to give your presentation...notice how calm you are...take a couple of long, slow deep breaths...and smile at your friends...feel that they are sending positive thoughts and energy your way...feel confident...look at the teacher...notice that the teacher is attentive...not threatening...look down at your cards...notice that the print is large and clear...introduce the topic and proceed to give your report...glancing at your notes...maintaining eye contact with the audience...listen to how clear and confident your voice sounds...(2 minute pause)...make your concluding statements...see the teacher smiling approval...answer any questions with clear, concise responses...return to your seat with a sense of satisfaction...see your grade in the teacher's book...feel proud that you did your best...keep this feeling with you as you return to the classroom...as I count to ten, begin to move your toes...1...2...3...4...your fingers...5...6...7...your arms and legs...8...9...10 and open your eyes.

PLAYWRITING IDEAS

PLAYWRITING is a very effective way to encourage creative writing because the final product is not something that will end up on the teacher's desk ready for the red pencil but a performance. I have yet to find a group of students, (preschool to graduate school) who do not enjoy writing and acting out plays. I've selected my favorite ideas and described them below:

FROM STORIES

When I first taught *Treasure Island* to my seventh graders, I discovered that they could barely get through the vocabulary let alone an entire chapter. Interest was dying fast so as a last ditch effort I broke the class into triads and told each group that all they had to do was read one chapter each. The group was responsible for: (1) Summarizing the main events of the chapter for the rest of the class (2) Providing a list of characters that appear in the chapter along with their roles (3) Acting out the events of the chapter for the class. They were limited to three people per group and had to devise ways to take all roles if more than three characters were needed. By the time all groups had gone once, they were ready and willing to take a second and third chapter to finish the story.

Because the pressure of reading the entire book was eliminated, students became enthusiastic. Little did they know that it was next to impossible to read only one chapter to get the background information that they needed! They were now reading with a new goal, so they did not mind that they had to read more. I allowed one week for all groups to prepare during class. This involved discussions of what props were needed, stage directions and dialogue to be included with the action. I encouraged students to write more dialogue than was in the story to make up for narration, which would be impossible with so few actors. The group sizes mandated that all members contribute.

This worked so well that I also tried it (successfully) with *Old Yeller*, *The Incredible Journey*, *Lord of the Flies*, and *Call of the Wild* as well as the writing of a final chapter to *Julie of the Wolves*. (It is especially interesting to see how students handle characters that are animals. Some tape the dialogue as if it is the thoughts of the animal and play it at the appropriate times in the action. Others use only actions and facial expressions to communicate.)

Writing and acting out plays is also a great alternative to oral book reports, challenging the student to portray one special scene with himself as the only actor available to play all parts!

FROM T.V. GUIDES

When it comes to writing an original story or play the problem always seems to be what to write about. I save the pages from T.V. guides that list the late night movies on Saturday and Sunday. These tend to be movies that very few have ever seen and there is quite a long list to choose from.

Again, I divide the class into groups and have them read over the blurbs. From these they can get a title, main character or two and an idea to be developed. It is just enough to get them started but not enough to stifle creativity. Taking a humorous approach the first time they do this will also make activity less threatening.

DEVELOPING THE ELEMENTS OF THE PLAY

Setting

Image each scene after deciding what action will be taking place. When it is a group project, individuals can image and then together fill in a MULTI-SENSORY CLUSTERING worksheet. This will also assist in making a list of sound effects and props needed. Once the scene has been mapped out on paper, again image it, this time watching for stage directions and location of props.

Dialogue

Once students have decided who will take the individual roles, suggest that they image themselves in the scene, reacting to the setting and other characters in a believable way. Have them write the dialogue after comparing ideas gotten from the imagery. Dialogue should always focus on either the action of the play or the inner thoughts and feelings of the characters. Imaging dialogue will also give ideas for *how* to speak, (i.e. dialects, accents, speech patterns).

Characters

Students may wish to use the CHARACTER DEVELOPMENT worksheet found in the Appendix to develop background information for the characters. Once the information is filled in, they can image to get ideas about how the character walks, talks, dresses, etc. Imaging the character being interviewed is another way to gain insights. You would ask the character about events in the story and listen to his thoughts and feelings about them.

Plot

Playing a game of *What if...* with the members of the group once the characters have been established, is a good way to get ideas for the plot. You may also wish to use the CAUSE AND EFFECT worksheet in the Appendix to plan out the action of the play. Begin with short vivid scenes and later elaborate if necessary to add to continuity or interest.

Stage Directions

Stage directions should be concise and should not be overused, that is, add stage directions only when the action needs further explanation, using as few words as possible. The best way to teach stage direction is to use other plays as models. Imaging the action while someone else reads the dialogue is an effective way to decide where to insert stage directions.

Because the worksheets mentioned are explained more fully in other sections, I have not gone into great detail about how to use them. Make the ideas presented here fit your needs and not visa versa.

SUGGESTED RESOURCES FOR WRITING PLAYS

A Play and Its Parts by Gerald Weales (Basic Books, 1964).

An Introduction To Playwriting by Samuel Selden (F.S. Crofts & Co., 1946).

Contemporary Children's Theater by Betty Jean Lifton (Avon Books, 1974).

Plays, the Drama Magazine for Young People (Plays, Inc., 8 Arlington St., Boston, MA 02116).

Playwriting: How To Write for Theater by Bernard Grebanier (Barnes and Noble, 1979).

Seven Plays and How to Produce Them by Moyne Rice Smith (Oxford University Press, 1968).

T.V. SCRIPTS

With the availability of video equipment in today's schools, you may wish to teach playwriting in conjunction with writing a shooting script for a T.V. show or commercial. *Brian's Song* and *The Miracle Worker* are excellent examples of T.V. playwriting and can be purchased in paperback for the class.

STORY IDEAS

I strongly suggest that you begin *small*...with commercials, public service announcements or news broadcasts. If you feel, however, that you wish to undertake a project that requires more time, (figure 1-2 minutes of tape = 1 ½ hours) then here are a few suggestions for the story line:
1. Develop a spinoff pilot show from a current series
2. Use a play already written and from that develop a shooting script
3. Use a short story as the basis for the show
4. Develop a game show from the ones now on the air
5. Retell a fairy tale, myth or fable
6. Take the main idea of a narrative poem and write it in play form
7. Use a human interest story from the newspaper to recreate events
8. Write a spoof episode of a soap opera
9. After viewing an episode of a running series, write the next week's show to follow—this will give students an idea of just how much work goes into each week's production
10. Prepare a documentary on the life of a famous author—include interviews

All of these ideas begin with a general cast of characters and story line. This will save time coming up with a completely new idea, and get you right into such matters as TREATMENTS and STORYBOARDS/SHOOTING SCRIPTS.

COMMERCIAL IDEAS

Here are a few ideas to get you started with writing original commercials. (It would be helpful if advertising techniques were introduced beforehand.)
1. Create a new product by combining aspects of things already on the market and then decide how you will advertise it. (For example, combining a copy machine with a truck could give you a vehicle that copies your route as you drive *to* a location and automatically gets you back home when you're ready to return.)
2. Write an ad to get financial backing for a school team.
3. Take the role of an author and try to sell your latest book
4. Write an ad to sell school lunches, text books or shares in the school system
5. Become a famous person and sell the key to your success. (For example, bottled beauty, a box of persistence or a pound of compassion.)

PUBLIC SERVICE ANNOUNCEMENTS/NEWS BROADCAST IDEAS

1. Use the daily newspaper for stories and/or topics (don't forget the editorials).
2. Report on a past historical event, myth, fable or fairy tale as if it were to happen today.

3. Research the causes of a major disaster from the past and create a public service announcement that may have changed the course of history for the better.
4. Create two broadcasts of the same event—one being objective and the other subjective.
5. Use school events as the subject of the broadcast.
6. Plan an interview with people who have opposing viewpoints on some topic to be reported. This idea can also be done with the characters from a story, each telling the story from his point of view.

WRITING A TREATMENT

The first step in a T.V. or movie production is the writing of a treatment. This is a brief plan of the content of the story, characters and setting for the shoot, etc. It is intended to make the production team, (writers, camera crew, sound and lighting technicians, actors and prop people) look at the project in general terms before they work out a shooting script/storyboard. Even a commercial that lasts only 30 seconds, should have a treatment.

I have made up a worksheet, WRITING A TREATMENT, and included it in the Appendix. This should be filled out after the group has had time to share their ideas with each other. A producer should be selected as the team's leader and should make all of the final decisions with regard to production. The shooting script/storyboard can be dealt with once the treatment has been completed.

SHOOTING SCRIPTS AND STORYBOARDS

Because shooting scripts and story boards contain similar information, I have combined directions for them. Basically, storyboards are composed of a series of illustrations of the key scenes mounted on a poster, while a shooting script is a more detailed description of each individual shot. The storyboard may contain drawings or photos and should be clear and concise, depicting from scene-to-scene what you want the viewer to see. Narrative and instructions for audio usually accompany the pictures. The SHOOTING SCRIPTS AND STORYBOARDS worksheet in the Appendix will be useful in planning a video production, even if you do not actually shoot it. If you wish students to make a storyboard, have them cut apart and mount in sequence, the boxes for each scene. Above each box, there should be a photo or sketch of the visual. For a shooting script, students will need several copies of the worksheet, but do not need a picture for each scene. I suggest keeping it simple, creating a storyboard with still shots. Use the activities below to plan each key scene and to demonstrate camera directions.

CAMERA DIRECTIONS

Image

You are going to become a video camera in order to experience the many different shots of which you are capable. Close your eyes and see yourself becoming a camera...your lens is your eye...adjust it so that you can see a rose bush off in the distance...you can see the entire bush...full of flowers...notice their colors...you can see things to the left and right of the bush...this is a long shot (LS)...PAN to the left, slowly...see what is to the left of the bush...now PAN back to the right...toward the bush...and pass by it...use a steady even motion...and stop the PAN on another object in the distance...the object will slowly become difficult to see as you FADE OUT to black...total darkness...when you FADE IN to the rose bush again you will be closer than you were last time...the bush now fills the entire frame...see the top...and bottom of the bush...notice that the individual flowers are easier to see...the colors are more vivid...ZOOM IN closer until all you can see is one flower..in this close-up (CU) of the flower you can see each petal...you can almost smell the nectar...ZOOM IN further for an extreme close-up (EXC) to see a drop of dew on the leaf...see how perfectly formed it is...now slowly ZOOM OUT...watching the flower getting smaller...until you can see the entire bush filling the frame once again...this is a medium shot (MS)...continue to ZOOM OUT until the bush is only a small speck in the distance...FADE OUT to black...bringing yourself back to the room on the count of ten...1-2-3-4-5-6-7-8-9-10.

Processing Out

Discuss the various camera shots and compare them.

Follow-Up

Watch T.V. while logging each type of shot used. The usual sequence is LS-MS-CU-LS-MS-CU-etc. Each time the shot changes, the angle also changes, (the camera moving to the right, left, up or down.) If video equipment is available, experiment with the shots; if it is not, try still shots with a camera or collect pictures from ads that demonstrate each shot.

PLANNING A SCENE

Image

(It may be helpful to review the TREATMENT before imaging.)

In order to create a storyboard, you will image each scene, seeing what the camera sees, paying attention to the audio and narration that go with it. We will image the first scene together. Each other following scene can be done in the same way. Go to your workshop to do the planning...look around when you get there and sit in a comfortable chair in front of the viewing screen...watch as the very beginning of the (story/commercial/documentary/interview) appears on the screen...read the title...notice the size and color of the letters...listen for the audio that goes with the title...and any narration...reverse the tape and see it play once again to be sure that you have not missed anything...continue to roll the tape as Scene 1 unfolds before you...listen to the actors speaking...watch the action...stop the tape when you come to the end of the scene...rewind the tape and watch it again to the end of scene one...take notes on what kind of camera shots were used...what the action was...what background music or sound effects were heard...when I count to five, open your eyes and fill in your shooting script worksheet...1-2-3-4-5.

Follow-Up

Continue imaging and developing the storyboard. Create a storyboard (using the worksheet) for a T.V. program/news broadcast/commercial.

GUIDELINES FOR VIDEO NARRATION

Narration for a video production is unique because it takes a back seat to what is seen on the screen. Here are some suggestions for writing a video narration:

1. *Write in conversation style*, the way people talk. (People do not always speak in complete sentences; instead they use single words or short phrases.) It should be natural and believable.

2. *Use simple language.* (News broadcasts use much simpler language than newspapers do. Try converting a news story into a news script.)
3. *Be direct.* Let the video tell the story. Don't describe things off the screen.
4. *Use evocative language.* The narration should be as lively and fast-paced as the video. Try using personification, alliteration, onomatopoeia, and metaphors.
5. *Use humor*, not gags or one liners, but rhyme, alliteration, plays on words, unexpected remarks, and surprise endings.
6. *Use effective transitions* between unrelated segments. Try to link segments that lack visual continuity.
7. *Don't tell exactly what the video is showing.* Narration should be a supplement to the video, filling in where there are pauses and elaborating on ideas.

SUGGESTED RESOURCES FOR VIDEOTAPING

Films

Televisionland. Pyramid Films. Color (12 minutes)

Basic Television Terms: A Video Dictionary. Pyramid Films. Color. (18 minutes)

The Making of a Live TV Show. Pyramid Films. Color. (26 minutes)

TV Behind the Screen. Churchill Films. Color. (15 ½ minutes)

Books/Articles

Anderson, J. and Ploughoff, M. *The Way We See It.* Dept. of Communication, University of Utah, Salt Lake City, UT 84112, 1978.

Singer, D., Singer, J., and Zuckerman, D. *Teaching Television.* N.Y.: Dial Press, 1981.

Fuller, B., Kanaba, S., and Kanaba, J. *Single-Camera Video Production.* Englewood Cliffs, NJ: Prentice-Hall, Inc. 1982.
Englander, D. and Gaskill, A. *How to Shoot A Movie Story.* NY: Morgan & Morgan, Inc. Pub., 1960.

Lewman, M. ''Writing Effective Narrations.'' *Educational and Industrial Television.* October, 1976 (48-50).

Szliak, D. ''There Is Writing and There Is Scriptwriting.'' *Educational and Industrial Television. May 1980, (71-73).*

Conradt, R. ''The Production Script.'' *Video Systems.* October, 1978, (36-38).

"Knowing anything in its deepest sense means knowing how to be creative with it.

—Elliot Eisner

CHAPTER EIGHT

Style

WARM-UPS

WHO AM I?

Have each student select a musical group and write a paragraph describing the style of music it records. Insist that the description focus on the music (lyrics, instrumentation, etc.) and not on the personalities of the members. Then read them aloud and have others try to guess the group. Follow up with descriptions of author's styles.

EMERGING STYLE

Listen to music recorded over a period of several years by the same artist. Then analyze the elements of style that have changed and those that have remained the same. Follow up with comparisons of works written by the same author over a period of years.

ADAPTING STYLE

After studying one author's style, have students rewrite a passage from a newspaper, magazine, poem, novel, etc. in that author's style. (For example, how would Jack London have written this poem?)

CREATING STYLES

Ask each student to write a brief description of a style that an author might use. (You may wish to discuss possibilities first.) Mix up the papers and distribute. Then assign students a topic to write on or a passage to rewrite, using the style described on the papers they've been given.

STYLE

An author's *STYLE* is his way of expressing his thoughts in writing. While one author may use terse sentences with simple vocabulary, another uses lengthy descriptive passages; one may write in a humorous tone while another is serious. Many authors (like musical groups) can be recognized through their styles.

The activities included in this chapter are provided not only to introduce the concept of style but to encourage students to experiment with and develop their own unique writing styles. You may wish to combine one of the style activities with an exercise from another chapter or as follow-up to another exercise. Experimenting with a variety of styles is also a way to *polish* a poem or story that seems to need that something extra. Many of the ideas provided can work with all types of writing, so they've been set apart for easy access. I encourage you to adapt the activities to fit your curriculum needs. The warm-up activities can also be effective as culminating exercises.

SCAVENGER HUNT

Procedure

Perhaps students can be encouraged to collect samples of the devices that make up an author's style. These samples can be added to a notebook or stored on the word processor over time. One of the best ways to internalize a concept is to search for, recopy, and store it for later reference. Samples located by the individual students often have more meaning to them personally. Having to recopy or memorize the model reinforces the distinction between styles.

In addition to the scavenger hunt for models, students can insert their best efforts at using each technique. The completed notebook becomes a personalized text.

(Don't forget to look for models in musical lyrics, historical documents, and advertisements.)

ALLITERATION

ALLITERATION is the repetition of a letter's sound for effect. These may be consonant or vowel sounds and are usually, but not always at the beginning of words.

ACTIVITY#1

Either brainstorm or cluster a letter of the alphabet to get a list of words that begin with that letter. Use these words to write tongue twisters.

ACTIVITY #2

Rewrite a sentence or short poem, substituting synonyms for as many words as is possible with the same beginning letter.

ACTIVITY #3

Write acrostic poems (see SELF IMAGE section) that employ alliteration in each line.
SAMPLE:
Jovival and Jolly
Outstandingly Outrageous
Sometimes sinister-looking when
Harassing hoary hyenas!

ACTIVITY #4

Each person in the class begins a sentence by writing the first word of it on a sheet of paper. Upon the signal from the teacher, students pass papers to someone else and add a word that continues the thought and repeats that sound. The procedure is repeated until all are complete; then read them aloud and laugh!

ACTIVITY #5

Using either the word cards or pictures from the picture file, have students write interesting descriptions. To encourage the use of evocative language, have dictionaries and thesauruses available. These descriptions or poems should not be corny tongue twisters, but make use of alliteration effectively. Imaging the object or scene before beginning writing will enhance the quality of the final product.

ONOMATOPOEIA

ONOMATOPOEIA is the imitation of natural sounds that produce an auditory image to the reader. (Such words as: hiss, rumble, screech, flop, etc. evoke auditory images of the objects producing them.)

ACTIVITY #1

Preparation

Distribute pictures from the picture file to each student. Allow students to become familiar with an object in the picture.

Image

Close your eyes and see the object of your picture…notice colors…shapes and sizes…watch it doing something typical for it to do…listen for the sounds that it makes…make the picture become black, as if you have turned out the lights…but continue to listen…notice how acute your hearing has become…you know exactly what is happening…focus on each sound…each rhythm…each movement…when you have a clear understanding of what's happening, open your eyes and prepare to write.

Write

Make a list of words that describe the actions of the object when heard in the dark. Try to be as evocative as possible (i.e. rather than *walk* use *shuffle* or *step-step-step*.) Keep your list in the sequence that the sounds were heard. Begin a new line to indicate a pause in the action. (i.e. *hop, hop, hop* indicates three quick hopes while *hop* on the first, second, and third lines shows that time passed between each hop.)

SAMPLE
*Purrrrrr
Purrrrrr
Scratch, scratch, scratch, scratch, scratch. scratch
Purrrrrrr

*The repetition of a letter at the end stretches both the sound and action for a clearer image.

The results of the writing can be called *Sound Poems* and left as is, or later be developed into vignettes.

ACTIVITY #2

Make word cards from the Onomatopoeia Word List (See Appendix), distribute several to each student and suggest that all words be used to describe a setting or character. In doing so, the underlying mood should emerge.

ACTIVITY #3

Repeat either of the above activities but focus on words that evoke tactile images (fluffy, scratchy, etc.) or olfactory images (putrid, salt-scented, etc.)

PERSONIFICATION

PERSONIFICATION is a figure of speech in which inanimate objects or beings less than human are given human actions, qualities, and/or characteristics.

ACTIVITY #1

Purpose

To personify emotions, describing them in relation to the effect they have upon people.

Preparation

Select an emotion that you will examine in the imagery. Write the words, *I am* , completing it with the emotion. (i.e. *I am fear*.) Put down your pencil, sit comfortably, and close your eyes.

Image

See a color that reminds you of the emotion...watch the color swirling around, slowly beginning to take on the shape of a being...see the size and color of the emotion...hear it speaking to you, telling you its name...watch how it moves...take note of where it lives...(longer pause)...observe what effect it has on people in a variety of situations...(longer pause)...before bringing your awareness back to the room, find out how it feels being that emotion...find out what makes this emotion's power fade...when I count to ten, open your eyes...1-2-3-4-5-6-7-8-9-10.

Write

Continue on the paper that you started earlier. Speak as if you are the emotion. Tell your innermost thoughts and feelings about who you are.

ACTIVITY #2

Purpose

To personify an object in an otherwise realistic situation.

Preparation

(Distribute pictures from the picture file.) Study your picture and find an object in it that you wish to personify. (pause)

Image

Now close your eyes and see the scene in the picture as if it is being projected onto a movie screen...watch what is happening in the scene...(longer pause)...now rewind the tape and play the same scene over again. This time zoom in on the object, listening to its thoughts and feelings while the scene plays...(longer pause)...give the object a personality...and a voice...when I count to five, open your eyes...1-2-3-4-5.

Write

Using the third person voice, describe the action in the scene. In a subtle way, personify the object of your focus as the scene unfolds.

SAMPLE:

The needle was waiting for the careless hands of a woman engrossed in her thoughts. When forced through the coarse material it rudely pierced the soft, pink flesh of her finger. She shuddered as the blood flickered red and oozed gently, cleansing the wound. Then she removed a cottonball from a cabinet, sponged up the drops of blood, and applied slight pressure. As she replaced the needle, it planned its next attack.

—Lisa Rachel Bein, Grade 9

ACTIVITY #3

Purpose

To personify a part of the body.

Procedure

When my seventh grade class did this, I asked them to select a part of their own bodies (i.e. hair, left hand, right foot, etc.) and keep a log for one day with regard to it (jotting down the things it did). They were to use this information to write a short story (in the first person) speaking as the body part, interjecting their emotions and thoughts with respect to things done to them, other body parts and the humans of whom they were a part. The suggested title was *A Day In The Life Of* ———————, but theirs were much more creative. Here are a few of them:

                    My Life as a Foot
                    My Many Adventures   by Erica Eye
                    Lucky Lips
                    Lee, the Knuckle

SIMILE

A *SIMILE* is a comparison made between two unrelated things through a common point using the words *like* (i.e. her long hair falls like a waterfall), *as* (i.e. busy as a bee), or *than* (i.e. her singing was sweeter than honey).

ACTIVITY #1

Purpose

To force comparisons of unlike things, using *like*, *as*, or *than*.

Procedure

Have students select two pictures each from the picture file and then write one sentence that compares an object in the first picture to something in the other. Comparisons may be based on such things as color, size, usage, movement, shape, etc.

Write

Follow up by rematching pictures and writing as many different similes as possible. Then select a favorite one and use it as the topic of an essay.

ACTIVITY #2

Purpose

To make a personal analogy, comparing oneself to something in nature.

Procedure

Ask students to find and bring into class, an object from nature. (It is not necessary that they know what it is for, the first time you do this activity.)

Write

Begin the first line with the words *I am like a*   , filling the blank with whatever the object is. Continue the essay by elaborating upon the introductory idea. A simple formula to follow might be:
Part 1: General comparison (The most striking similarity)
Part 2: Specific comparisons that elaborate upon the first general idea.
Part 3: Restating the general comparison.

ACTIVITY #3

Purpose

To use imagery to brainstorm similes.

Procedure

Students will be given the first part of a simile and be asked to image and write as many different endings as possible. It is important to allow enough time for the image-write-image-write process to take place. Simply repeat the partial simile several times before going on. Encourage several responses for each. Here are a few to get you started:

Simile Beginnings:

As dirty as a ———

As white as ———

As peaceful as ———

Strength like ———

Faster than ———

As honest as ———

Simile Endings:

——— like a fox.

——— as a balloon.

——— like oil.

——— than the wind.

——— like music.

——— as a turtle's shell.

Later students should go back and select a few from their lists and elaborate on them. This can be in the form of long descriptive sentences, paragraphs, or poems.

METAPHOR

A *METAPHOR* is a direct comparison between two unlike things. In *His hair is a mop*, *his hair* is called the *TENOR* (the thing being compared) and *a mop* the *VEHICLE* (the thing to which it is compared).

ACTIVITY #1

Repeat the simile activities stressing that the words *like*, *as*, and *than* may not be used.

ACTIVITY #2

Purpose

To write comparisons of unlike things when given either the *TENOR*, *VEHICLE*, or both.

Preparation

Color code index cards for *TENOR* and *VEHICLE* suggestions. (Below are some to get you started.) Have students select one card and use that suggestion to write a metaphor. Later one of each card may be used to create a *forced* comparison. The key to success is *using verbs* to make the *VEHICLE do* something or *act* in some way. Note that some suggestions are general. When writing metaphors use a specific example.

TENOR CARDS	VEHICLE CARDS
Feeling of joy	An animal
Feeling of pride	A piece of music
Feeling of fear	A work of art
Doing something difficult	A weather condition
Doing something easy	A flower
Doing something selfish	Playing
Friend	Fishing
A teacher	Designing
A Pet	Travelling
A Hero	A household item
Life	A tool
Peace	An object in nature
War	

Image

Here, autonomous imaging works best. Suggest that students image what is on the card first, write down some ideas (perhaps clustering the card's main idea) and image again to decide the most effective comparison.

SYNAESTHESIA

SYNAESTHESIA refers to a crossing of sensory experiences so that, for example, what you have heard is described instead as something you have seen, tasted, touched, or smelled. This technique creates interest because it contradicts what we normally believe to be true.

ACTIVITY

Purpose:

To experiment with discrepant sensory descriptions.

Procedure:

Using the *Multi-sensory Clustering* worksheet (APPENDIX) cluster as you normally would, using a picture, imaged scene, or recorded sounds as the focus.

Write

Explain to students that they must describe the scene using the ideas on the worksheet. They must, however, use a sense other than the one in whose section the idea is written. If *darkness* is written in the *see* section, than rather than *seeing darkness*, they must hear, smell, taste or touch it.

SYNECHDOCHE and METONOMY

SYNECHDOCHE takes the most dramatic part of a thing to stand for the thing itself. *METONOMY* uses an attribute or object closely associated with a more comprehensive term, itself. Using the word *throne* or *crown* to represent the government is metonomy; Housman's use of *homespun hearts* to represent the whole being of rustic Englishmen was synecdoche.

ACTIVITY

Purpose

To brainstorm possible substitutions for words (nouns) used in writing.

Procedure

Have the class brainstorm a list of nouns and put them on the board. Next, divide the class into groups and ask each if they can come up with words or phrases to take the place of the nouns on the board. The substitutions they write should either be a dramatic representation of the word listed or an attribute closely associated with it. Suggest that they elaborate whenever possible.

To test their success, groups should read what they've written aloud and ask the class to guess which term it stands for. You can also categorize responses as synechdoche or metonomy.

APOSTROPHE

APOSTROPHE is addressing a non-living person (historical figure, relative, etc.) or personified abstraction (science, art, war, etc.). When using apostrophe, the writer's innermost thoughts can be shared freely because the one being addressed cannot hear or respond.

ACTIVITY

Purpose

To share thoughts/ideas in a letter to someone who cannot/will not receive it.

Procedure

This is one of the most powerful activities you can do with your students when the addressee is a personal friend or relative. Moving away from the above definition, somewhat, I ask students to write a letter to someone telling him/her something that they cannot say in person. This may be because the person is dead, but can be someone that they just cannot possibly address person-to-person.

Writing the letter can be extremely therapeutic; reading letters aloud can be extremely threatening. Use caution if sharing is done. Some students may be unable to read theirs aloud. Encourage humor the first time you do this, then go to more serious content.

SAMPLE:

To: Miss Dorothy E. Thompson, Teacher
Somewhere in Heaven
Dear Miss Thompson,

I hope you remember me. I was that very shy, extremely quiet, pudgy, pig-tailed Indian girl in your fourth and fifth grade class in Midlothian, Illinois more than forty years ago. Nowadays, Miss Thompson, a kid can't have the same teacher for two years in a row, but back then, I was happy to know that you would be my fifth grade teacher. I loved you.

You taught me basic skills, but I forgot how you did that. I remember: planting seeds in a bread box filled with moistened soil, placing them in a dark closet, and checking for sprouts; I remember a Sioux Indian chief visiting our classroom; I remember you showing us how to draw figures in motion on an ice-skating pond, by penciling in simple geometric shapes before we drew in crayon or chalk; I remember your liking my story about the Norwegian pianist who sent messages to the underground by the music he played and how he played it; I remember the fun we had when Larry Sargent, the local funeral director's son, and his buddies presented a weekly serial with clay puppets every Friday afternoon. Those puppets usually lost their heads or limbs in the course of each adventure, and how we laughed!

I can still see your signature, Miss Thompson. It was clear, beautiful, and yet different from the script you taught us. On our report cards you always inserted your middle initial—E. Your signature was just like you—tiny, direct, and neat.

You don't know this, but several years later I chanced to see you on a train somewhere between Beloit, Wisconsin, and Chicago, Illinois. (I had heard that you had left our little hamlet and gone on to a better position.) I was in college then, and together with friends, I was heading for a good time in the Windy City. Walking through the train with a friend, I saw you. You didn't recognize me, and I wasn't certain that you were you. You wore makeup, you were very well-dressed, and you had a book open in your lap. You were chatting with your companions, and you were laughing. I nudged my friend and said, "Don't look now, but that's my old teacher!"

Forgive me, Dorothy. You must have been under forty when I uttered those words. Now, I too am an *old teacher*. I like the feeling. Thanks for everything.

Love,
Ida Powlas (Moore)

RHYTHM

Although more obvious in poetry, prose too, makes use of the RHYTHMIC FLOW of language to create a sense of continuity and wholeness in the writing. Rhythm may be created by the repetition of a letter sound (alliteration), word or phrase (recurrence) or groups of phrases (parallel form). Rhyme also can create rhythm.

Rhythm is an innate part of us. It was the beating of our mothers' hearts before we were born, the babbling chants of our first spoken language. Being rocked, sung to and read to all reinforced the pleasure of rhythm. Even young children are aware of the rhythm of language. I witnessed this first hand when my youngest son, Dustin, was learning to say his bedtime prayers. He was about three at the time and for several nights in a row did not include his name at the end of the list of family members following the words, *God bless....* I finally asked him why he stopped with his brother Joshua's name. "My name doesn't fit," was his response.

Sure enough, when I looked at the rhythm of the prayer and the way it was spoken, the extra syllables at the end didn't fit. By shortening Joshua to Josh, Dustin liked the sound of it better. It fit!

By experimenting with rhythm in writing, individual styles really begin to emerge. Rhythm is not something to be taught but something to be felt.

ACTIVITY #1

MEMORIZATION of a variety of styles is the best way to *feel* rhythm. Poems are the best place to start. For longer poems, I suggest a verse a day or just the first stanza. Begin class by listening to several students repeat the same poem. (I call on the ones who know it best, first. This helps the others by hearing it several more times before they must recite.) Having students select a favorite poem is a good way to begin. Start with shorter rhyming poems to build up their confidence and later try longer ones.

ACTIVITY #2

Take a familiar tune and have students write a PARODY for it. They will be forced to focus on the rhythm of the melody as well as the theme of the original words. Humorous songs are fun and groups of students usually don't mind performing their song for the rest of the class. There are many hit songs today that have inspired the writing of a parody.

Here is a parody that was written by six teachers. It is sung to the tune of *The Twelve Days of Christmas*.

The Twelve Days of Teaching

1984
By Barbara DeLong, Ina Sinovoi, Dorothy Ramundo, Peter Derven, Marguerite Deacon, & Helen Spagnolo

On my first day of teaching
My principal gave to me
A class load intended for three*...

On my second day of teaching
My Principal gave to me
Two hyperactives...

On my third day of teaching
My principal gave to me
Three lunchroom duties...

On my fourth day of teaching
My principal gave to me
Four open houses...

On my fifth day of teaching
My principal gave to me
Five behavioral objectives...

On my sixth day of teaching
My principal gave to me
six irate parents...

On my seventh day of teaching
My principal gave to me
seven observations...

On my eighth day of teaching
My principal gave to me
eight hulking fullbacks...

On my ninth day of teaching
my principal gave tome
nine femme fatales...

On my tenth day of teaching
My principal gave to me
ten pregnant freshmen...

On my eleventh day of teaching
my principal gave to me
Eleven senseless meetings...

On my twelfth day of teaching
My principal gave to me
twelve nervous breakdowns...

*Final verse replaces "And a class load intended for three" with "And a contract to sing in Italy."

ACTIVITY #3

FREE ASSOCIATION, similar to clustering in that it produces a free flow of ideas, can be used to create rhythm in poetry or prose. It is a prewriting activity that generates a word list. I usually begin with word cards but students can simply select a word with which to begin. That word is written at the top left of the page. Under it is the first word that comes to mind; under that word, is written the next word triggered by the last word written. This procedure is continued until there are about four columns of words on the page (about 10 minutes). When a new word does not come, I tell students to continue to write the last word over and over again until a new thought comes to mind. The pens should not stop moving while they *think* of the next word. There is no thinking allowed! They are to write—not examine.

A variation to the writing of the same word until a new one pops into their minds is to have students write the original word over and over again until a new idea comes. This also may happen naturally—coming back to the original theme as an idea is exhausted.

Students can use these lists to write poems or essays. The lists will be full of synonyms and multiple meanings.

ACTIVITY #4

RECURRENCES of specific words and phrases can be a powerful device. Repetition creates emphasis, both on the sound rhythm of the writing and the meaning. Even the placement of the repeated words is important. In the samples below, you can see the effect that the recurrences has. The key to deciding whether or not to use the same word or to use a synonym is *felt* in both the rhythm and the meaning to be conveyed.

SAMPLES:

Nervous
 by Laura A. Gebhart, Gr. 11

Pacing, pacing, pacing
Wringing hands
Biting bottom lip
Talking to no one
Pacing, pacing, pacing...

Pen Feelings
 by Paul Yankalunas, Gr. 7

I wonder if they like it being pens?
I suppose they don't.

Having to look at businessmen
They get pushed and mistreated
No wonder why
Because of people
Like you and I.

And when you are done
We get thrown away
And you, too would get sick of this
Day after day after day...

Imperfection
 by Jonathan Feist, Gr. 9

The plane is black
That is all it is
Black
No color, not even a slight mar
Black as a starless night
Black as only nothingness can be
Black
Not a trace of light
Perfectly
Black.

But wait. . .
A speck of dust
A faint glimpse of light
All that is needed
To make something once divine, once pure
Marred
Imperfect
Ruined
No longer purely
Black.

ACTIVITY #5

Using PARALLEL FORM means to let words and phrases seek their own kind—noun to noun, verb to verb, phrase to phrase. Use of parallel form creates a pattern and thus creates rhythm. (In the last sample poem, Jonathan also made use of parallel form.)

One way to practice the use of parallel form is to cluster to generate ideas and then, while writing, look for ways to use 2-3 ideas from the cluster together in a series. Putting the ideas in the same sentence forces the writer to use similar phrasing and/or suffixes.

For example:

The writing:
I'm afraid of witches with bubbling brews, of wizards with wicked spells and of goblins with black cats. (nouns are all plural, phrases begin with with)
I'm afraid of being in the dark, being alone, being by myself. (phrases begin with 'being')

I'm afraid of screaming wind, screeching owls and especially of creaking floors. (adjectives all have 'ing' suffix)

"Most adults have lost the capacity to tell a good story. A good storyteller follows internal sights, sounds and movements. A nonimager knows what is important and can recite general principles but has difficulties describing the particulars, which are the basis of a good story."

—Robert Sommer

CHAPTER NINE

Fiction

WARM-UPS

LITERATURE NOTEBOOK

As suggested in the chapter on style, collect sample passages and titles that exemplify each element of literature being studied, including original samples as well. This can serve as a reference book when studying or doing future writing.

INTERESTING OPENERS

After perusing a variety of books with differing themes and styles, divide the class into groups to write as many opening lines to stories as they can, putting them on 3x5 cards. Later you may wish to make the cards available to students for spontaneous story-making activities. (The key here is variety—use both first and third person; past, present, and future tenses; humorous and serious tones; and imaginary and realistic themes.)

STRING STORY

Distribute 3x5 cards to students (sitting in a circle). Instruct them to write any word or phrase on the card (large enough to be seen by all) and hold up toward the center of the circle. The teacher holds a ball of string and, while sitting in the circle, begins to tell a story. As soon as he/she can connect the story line to what is on *any* card being held, both the ball of string and the responsibility to continue the story goes to that student. Continue until all cards have been included. Students enjoy tossing the ball of string and *only* the one handling it may speak.

STRING STORY VARIATION

Each student goes to the board and writes a word or phrase. When the list is complete, all students write original stories using the same beginning but the listed words in any way they wish. All enjoy hearing the outcomes.

FORMULAS

Many of the formulas found in the chapter on poetry can be used to write about setting, characters, or theme. Try using the formulas to capture the essence of the element being developed before transposing it to prose. (Using pictures from the Picture File is a good way to get started.)

SETTING

The *SETTING* tells when and where a story takes place. Settings may be real or imaginary; past, present, or future; spanning a brief moment or the lifetime of a character. Often it is the setting which helps to create the mood.

ACTIVITY #1

Purpose

To create a description of a setting.

Materials

Multi-sensory Clustering Worksheet (see Appendix) and Picture File.

Preparation

Ask each student to select a picture of a setting and begin to fill in information about the setting in the Multi-sensory Clustering Worksheet. Wait about three minutes before imaging.

Image

Put your pencils down and get into a comfortable position. Close your eyes and see yourself at the place in the picture...scan the entire area to see everything there is to see...(longer pause)...listen to the sounds here...smell the air...notice the time of day...and how you are feeling in this place...tune in to the mood of your surroundings...when you feel you know the setting as if you had really visited it, open your eyes and add any new ideas to the cluster. In the center describe the mood created by the setting.

Write

When the cluster is complete, use the ideas to write a descriptive paragraph about this place. Length is not as important as the use of evocative language.

SAMPLE

Scorching the desert, the sun shone brightly
as the wind threw sand across the land.
Warily approaching a damp pool, a rabbit
quickly darted away from the jagged teeth
of a snake. In the hazy sky, a vulture was
flying across the bleak, sizzling desert.

Davidd Levy, Grade 9

127

ACTIVITY #2

Purpose

To create a believable setting for a character.

Materials

Picture File featuring characters or an already developed character profile.

Image

Close your eyes and see your character in your mind's eye. Notice how the character is dressed...from head ...to toe...take a guess as to the time period the character is living in from the clothing worn...see the character doing something...noticing where it is being done...scan the area to the right of the character...and then to the left...(longer pause)...see if there are other people here...listen for sounds...smell the air...notice the character's mood...read the character's thoughts about this place...(longer pause)...when I count to five open your eyes...1...2...3...4...5.

Write

Write a description of the setting as seen through the thoughts and actions of the character. Use either first or third person.

SAMPLE

Taking the flickering torch, the knight walked down the bleak corridor. When he opened the door, he saw a dank room with a pool in the center. He submerged the torch into the raw water and felt his hand numb. Suddenly, a shrill screech shattered the air. As he tried to pull out the piercing icicles from his chest, he realized his body was becoming frostbitten and slowly sulked down into the corner of the room.

    Davidd Levy Gr. 9

Another way to describe the setting is to begin with the character's overall feeling of the place and then use detailed sentences describing how things feel, look, sound, and smell. Comparisons are encouraged.

CHARACTERIZATION

The *CHARACTER* in a story is the central figure. Usually characters are human, but can be animals or personified objects. The character's personality is revealed to the reader through his actions and thoughts as well as how others react to him. Whether realistic fiction or fantasy, the character must be believable.

ACTIVITY #1

Purpose

To develop a story line around an animal character.

Materials

Animal to observe—either a pet, wild animal, zoo animal, or pet shop animal. (Use pictures as a last resort.)

Preparation

Instruct students to find an animal to observe. As they watch, they should take notes on such things as physical appearance, manner of movement, and typical actions. After at least five minutes of observation, tell students to begin to let their minds wander—placing the animal in a different setting or situation for a story.

Image

Autonomously image this idea for several minutes.

Write

Write the opening paragraph to a story, using the animal as the focus. Let the descriptions of the animal character create interest by suggesting the story to be told.

SAMPLE

(This sample was written after a few minutes of observing one of my pet Springer Spaniels):
I watched Shadow, our black and white Springer, sprawled by the wood stove. On the floor, beads of dirty water encircled one paw where the frozen chunks had clung to his hair and swollen pads. His sides heaved rhythmically, the skin stretching over his ribs with each rising motion. He was finally asleep; finally home.

ACTIVITY #2

Purpose

To personify an object and make it the character in a story.

Materials

Each student should select one object from his/her home. If the background about the object is unknown, students should question family members or look up information about it. Antiques and family *treasures* are especially good objects to use.

Preparation

Begin by having students select an object and gather information about it. Age, use, construction, ownership, etc. will be helpful.

Image

You are going to become the object from your home and image its life story. Close your eyes and see yourself being constructed...becoming the object...notice the kind of craftsmen that make objects such as you are...(longer pause)...observe every detail of yourself as you become finished...and the proud smile of the one who has made you...follow your lifestory...as it plays for you like a movie...follow yourself, as the object, through all of the important events that led up to it being where it is today...(2-5 minute pause)...as I count to ten, remember the most significant happenings of your life as this object...1...2...3...etc.

Write

Tell your life story in the form of a diary or story. Focus on feelings as well as events. Select one major event of your life and write a story in the first person telling about it.

ACTIVITY #3

Purpose

To develop a character's background before writing a story. (Also: to collect background information while reading a story in class.)

Materials

Character Development Worksheet (see Appendix) and Picture File.

Preparation

Instruct students to use as the starting focus, a character in the picture selected. Begin to fill in any information on the Character Development Worksheet, beginning with the physical characteristics. Make up a name, etc. and fill in. Allow for about 5-10 minutes before imaging.

Image

Whether or not you have filled in all the information, put your pencil down. You are now going to image the character to gain new insights. Close your eyes...and see the character in the picture...pretend that you are a newspaper reporter, ready to interview the character...as you approach, scan the setting...the character looks up at you...and introduces him or herself...notice the voice tone...study the facial features...ask a question about the character's family background...listen to the response...(longer pause)...watch the character move...continue to ask questions, mentally taking notes as the character speaks...(longer pause 2-3 minutes)...watch as the character seems to drift away in thought...guess at what the character might be thinking...say good-bye...and bring your awareness back to the classroom as I count to ten...1...2...3...etc.

Write

Fill in any new information on the worksheet. Then write the opening paragraphs to a story—enough to establish interest in the character, but not necessarily the entire story. Speak as the character spoke to you in the interview—in first person, present tense. Begin with *My name is* and continue to tell the beginning of a very personal story. You do not need to use all the information on the worksheet. Use what is most important and most interesting.

A variation to the writing is to write in the third person. Students who find it difficult to become the character should be encouraged to use third person instead. Here the interviewer can interject personal thoughts, but write as if for a magazine interview feature. For example:

Can A Straight Rock Star Make It In Today's World?

Recently, famed rock singer Kate Mulligan was involved in a drug bust at a party following one of her concerts. Seeing her frail body curled up on the sofa of her N.Y.C. apartment, surrounded by art deco and hanging plants, I wondered at the contrast of this image to the wild antics so often associated with today's music business and its prima donna musicians.

ACTIVITY #4

Purpose

To describe a character showing a contrast or change that has taken place.

Materials

Picture File (optional)

Preparation

Use either a Character Development Worksheet, character from a story read in class, or character from the picture file to write about.

Image

Autonomously image the character as a youth. Slowly watch the character age and change.

Write

In a paragraph, try to show the most dramatic effects of the change upon the character.

SAMPLES

Etched in between the deep wrinkles of her face were two sad brown eyes which were yearning for the joys of seeing young children laughing and playing. Frail little hands pulled a ragged old shawl tighter around her shoulders as fond memories made her shiver. As parched lips opened they revealed a toothless smile. She began speaking in a wheezing whisper—telling her grandchild's favorite bedtime story—even though she knew no one was there to listen.
   Michele Helfand, Grade 9

The old man was shuffling across the floor. The years showed in his face. Wrinkles surrounded his eyes, which once sparkled with joy. His bald head had a few white hairs left. His eyes showed depression and sadness. As he tried to stand, but couldn't, he felt frustrated. The words no longer came easily to him. He wanted to talk, but just found it too difficult. His mind wasn't working the way it used to either. When he couldn't remember something he got upset. Once, while walking home, he forgot the way. It scared him; he had been going that way for years. He never thought he'd be this way, but what was the other choice. The child he once carried now helped him as he climbed the stairs.
   Robin Schiff, Grade 9

Image

Autonomously image the character as you have developed him/her. Slowly see another, more subtle side of the character emerge.

Write

In a paragraph, try to show the subtle contrasting side of the character's personality.

SAMPLES

Immersed in the thunderous downpour, his pointed countenance reflected an unjustly cruel childhood, filled with many unhappy memories. His glowing eyes seemed flecked with hatred towards mankind as he gruffly smashed his way through the bitter crowd. Spying a helpless kitten, he bent down, extending a trembling frostbitten hand. Slowly and gently he caressed the animal, his face breaking into an uncertain smile.
   Kim Tirone, Gr. 9

The young woman sat on the park bench alone. Physically she was perfect. When her eyes were averted, her glossy black hair and ivory skin received more than their fair share of admiring glances from eligible bachelors. Yet when her eyes met those of a bypasser, a piercing gleam of bitterness was revealed. The feelings behind those icy, dark, frozen pools were clearly barren of sparkle and glow. What had happened to make her so full of stinging hate?
   Linda Schatten, Grade 9

Image

Autonomously image the character as you have developed him/her. This time go back in time to discover an event or circumstance that has contributed to the present condition or state of mind.

Write

In a paragraph describe the character's current state alluding to the cause of it.

SAMPLE

A slight, frail body is shuffling along the streets of the ghetto, shivering in the cold, bitter evening. Large, watery eyes, clouded with misery, mournfully survey the dismal surroundings. Cruel barbed wire stares back at him. He sniffles occasionally, his racking cough shattering the night. Small hands once baby soft are now gruff from the cold and hard work. His dreams are shattered, his freedom wrenched heartlessly from him. The garish yellow star pinned to ragged clothing flutters in the breeze.
Gail A. Katz, Grade 9

Image

Select a character from a story and autonomously image the character as he/she appears at the beginning, middle and end of the story. Rereading passages before you image is helpful.

Write

Use three descriptive sentences to show how the character has changed. Try to vary language (especially nouns used to describe the character) to show the transition.

SAMPLE

(Call of the Wild)
The strongly muscled moose, an arrow piercing his shoulder, strolled as though he was a king among the cows.
The struggling half-ton beast's eyes widened, smoke streaming from his nose as he stomped, trying to give the fanged animal a blow on the head.
The dying animal drooling and gasping for breath, never once allowed to fulfill his appetite, knew he was defeated.
Christina Bonner, Grade 7

ACTIVITY #5

Purpose

To create a character sketch in a visual rather than written format. (Also: to describe a character from a story read in class.)

Materials

Old magazines to cut. Character Descriptors Worksheet (optional—see Appendix).

Procedure

Either brainstorm words that could be used to describe personality traits or use the Character Descriptors Worksheets and have students circle 10 words. These will describe the character to be developed. Once completed, students should begin to search for pictures that exemplify each trait. (For example, adventurous could be a picture of skydiving.) Use pictures to make a mobile or montage for the character.

Write

As a follow-up to the montage, students could write about events depicted in the pictures. Making a time line first will help to organize events and ideas.

PLOT

The events surrounding the character are the *PLOT*. Events may be introduced in any order but should be planned out in advance on a time line.

ACTIVITY #1

Purpose

To develop a story line using objects.

Materials

Odds and ends are great to use. Ask students to bring in a piece of *junk* (something no longer needed).

Procedure

From what is collected, select 4 to 6 objects (i.e. ticket stub, hat, old battery, paper clip, and broken scuba mask). (Save the rest for another time.) Tell students to assume that these belong to the main character of the story. They reveal information about the character and setting and may be used as significant parts of the story.

In small groups, use the objects to tell a story. Once the story line is decided upon, the group must tell its story to the class, each taking a part in some way.

ACTIVITY #2

Purpose

To use character descriptions to define the plot.

Preparation

After developing a character, decide what event will be written about after the character is introduced.

Image

See the character in the setting you have created...freeze the picture...and scan it for every little detail in terms of what the character is doing and what might happen next...(longer pause)...continue the action as you would a movie...stop...and rewind...play back the opening scene again...when I count to three, open your eyes...1...2...3.

Write

Describe the opening scene. Keep the mood strong. Let it lead into the impending action.

135

SAMPLE

The doberman was standing at a bitter halt. His ears were spikes of anger and from his mouth dripped the blood of his last attacker. The pincher was waiting for someone to pierce the silence of the night so he could spring upon the foe. Since his glowing black and brown coat was easily visible, not many people would dare come close in fear of death!
  Oren Warter, Grade 9

ACTIVITY #3

Purpose

To use the descriptions of the setting to define the plot.

Procedure

Same as for character. Writing should emphasize the mood and lay the groundwork for things to come.

SAMPLE

  A sharp scream pierced the night.
Flames crackled like fingers of death.
Wood hissed and water hit scorched wood.
Icicles formed in the frigid air.
The night was a bloody confrontation between hot and cold.
  Daniel Kaplan, Gr. 9

ACTIVITY #4

Purpose

To use the newspaper to get ideas for stories.

Materials

Newspapers and 3x5 cards.

Procedure

Scan news articles to find stories of personal interest to students. When each student has selected a story, have him write a brief description of the setting, characters, and plot on the 3x5 card.
  From this point there are several things that can be done, including:
  A Multi-sensory Clustering for the setting after imaging;
  A character development for the main character after imaging;
  Developing the events that led up to the article being written;
  Developing the events that will follow the events in the article;
  A time line of events using the Cause and Effect Worksheet. (See Appendix)

Write

Some of the options are:

Write a short story or play about the events that are written about in the article.

Write a short story about the events that led up to the article in the paper.

Write a short story about the events that occurred after the article appeared in the paper.

SAMPLE SHORT STORY

I have included a sample short story that makes use of imaging to develop the setting, main character, and plot. Each activity should be done separately in the suggested order. Discussion, if class time allows for it, is a good way to end the setting and character imageries. The actual writing does not begin until all of the imaging activities are completed, although there is note-taking and clustering suggested in order to assist keeping track of ideas along the way. Usually five class sessions are necessary to complete the story.

The students will be creating a setting and main character and then become an observer as a crime is being committed. They will be aware of their own reactions to the conflict as the story unfolds in the imagery and use this information when writing their *eye witness* accounts.

SETTING ACTIVITY (DAY 1)

Purpose

To create a believable present-day setting for a story where a crime will take place.

Materials

Phone directory with yellow pages.

Preparation

Blindly open the phone directory to the yellow pages and point to any ad. This information will be the basis for your setting. Copy down whatever is given in the ad before imaging.

Image

You will be creating a scene and place from which to view the action of the story. Read over the information you've written down about the place of business. Close your eyes and see this place...read the sign with the name on it...notice what the sign is made of and where it is on the building...examine the building and take a guess as to its age...look to the right, noticing what is located there...(longer pause)...and now to the left...(longer pause)...walk slowly to the door...listen to and feel the door as you open it...enter the building and notice what strikes you as you enter...(longer pause)...now, like a movie camera, pan in slow motion, taking in the entire scene...(longer pause)...take in every detail...face the door now from the inside...and leave the building...notice what is located directly in front of you...you may see something that you did not notice before...now that you are familiar with this scene, select a place where you can observe the action of the story...and go there now...it may be a park bench across the street, riding by on a bus, or a place inside the building...anywhere you wish to be that you feel comfortable...(longer pause)...once at your point of observation, scan the scene from this location...when I count to ten open your eyes...1...2...3...etc.

Write

Draw a map or floor plan of the scene. Jot down any notes, as a cluster or multi-sensory cluster. Fill in any details that will help you to remember the images.

138

CHARACTER ACTIVITY (DAY 2)

Purpose

To create a believable character for the crime story.

Materials

Phone directory and Character Development Worksheet. (see Appendix)

Preparation

Tell students to open the phone directory to any page and select a name. Tell them to write that in the appropriate space on the Character Development Worksheet and put their pens down.

Image

See the character's name on a mailbox…now move from the mailbox to the character's front door…notice the kind of front door it is…and the rest of the building…enter the character's home…observing the style and color of the furniture…(longer pause)…take a guess at the character's education and profession from what you see in his or her home…(longer pause)…wander through the home searching for clues that tell you more about the character and the character's family…(longer pause)…now see the character leaving the home…notice how the character is dressed…follow the character through a typical day…noting people met…places visited…and anything else of interest…(pause 2-3 minutes)…When I count to ten, bring your awareness back to the classroom…1…2…3…etc.

Write

Complete the Character Development Worksheet.

PLOT ACTIVITY (DAY 3)

Purpose

To combine the character and setting with a problem and eventual solution to it.

Preparation

Reread the information you've written about the character and setting so far.

Image

After reviewing information about the character, close your eyes and see the character talking on the phone…you are about to overhear the character discussing a crime to be committed…you will only hear bits of the conversation…not all of it…you must guess at who is at the other end…try to figure out what's about to take place and how the setting will fit into the total picture…(longer pause)…try to think of ways that you might foil this plan…(longer pause)…notice how you feel about the crime to be committed...(longer pause)...now go to the place you've selected in the setting to observe the action...notice what time of day it is...observe signs around you that tell what time of year it is...next watch, as you would a movie as the story takes place...pay attention to the actions of the characters as well as what they might be thinking...(pause 3-5 minutes)...as I count to ten, review the main events of the story...1...2...3...etc.

Write

Cluster the word "crime" or just jot down any notes and ideas that came to you during the imagery. Include your reactions and thoughts in a second cluster for the word "reactions".

PUTTING IT ALL TOGETHER (DAYS 4 AND 5)

Purpose

To use the information from the prewriting activities to write a short story.

Preparation

Reread and revise any of the notes taken.

Image

Autonomously image the story again.

Write

Tell your story as an eye witness in the first person. Write as if you are telling a close friend immediately after the crime took place. Maintain the energy of the emotions you felt at the time as you speak, interjecting your own thoughts throughout.

FANTASY

A *FANTASY* is a story that contains imaginary characters, setting, events, or any combination of the three.

ACTIVITY

Purpose

To use plot ideas taken from news articles to create a fantasy story.

Materials

Use newspapers to find ideas (see PLOT ACTIVITIES) or use the Plot Ideas Worksheet (see Appendix).

Procedure

Ask groups of students to select a plot idea that appeals to them. They should then brainstorm ways to make the setting unreal; then the characters unreal; and lastly, the events of the plot unreal.

Write

Using the three lists, the group should then select the most interesting combination and write a fantasy story based upon the original story line. (The story could follow the guidelines for either a fable, tall tale, or myth as well.)

FABLES

A *Fable* is a short fantasy story that teaches a lesson. Most characters in fables are animals which talk.

ACTIVITY #1

Purpose

To write a short story to teach a lesson.

Materials

Reference books for fables.

Procedure

Before writing fables, students should read and / or hear a variety of fables. Since the key to a fable is a lesson to be learned, students can make a list of lessons taught by the fables they've read.

Write

Using the list of lessons from stories, ask students to select one and write a new fable to teach the same lesson, changing first, the animal characters.

ACTIVITY #2

Purpose

To write a fable after deciding upon what lesson you'd like to teach others.

Preparation

Students will image themselves becoming wise animals with a need to teach an important lesson to someone.

Image

In this imagery you will become any animal that you wish...close your eyes...and look into the mirror...watch your face beginning to transform...you are becoming an animal...a leader of your kind...wise...strong...and proud...you are respected by other animals for your wisdom...it is your job to travel through the animal kingdom...when you see a problem, think of a way to demonstrate to the other animals how it can be solved...(longer pause)...when you see foolishness, think of a way to teach a lesson through it...(longer pause)...when you feel you've gotten an idea for a fable, bring your awareness back to the room and begin to write.

Write

Write a fable using the third person. Keep it brief and simple. End with a summary statement of the lesson taught. Remember to have animal characters behaving as humans. Illustrate your fable if you wish.

MYTHS

MYTHS are stories that explain natural happenings in the world. Mythology was a religion for early civilizations (Egyptians, Greeks, Romans, Norseman, Chinese, Eskimos, Hispanics, Japanese, Polynesians, to name a few). Myths tell us a great deal about what qualities we admire and unknowns that we fear in the world.

ACTIVITY #1

Purpose

To become familiar with Greek/Roman Mythology.

Materials

Reference books on Mythology or you may distribute copies of the Chart of Greek and Roman Mythology (see Appendix). Once the students have become familiar with the names and positions, they may wish to do one or all of the writing suggestions.

Write

Make a family tree for the gods and goddesses. (My fifth grade class handled this easily when working in groups.)

—Write a letter to Zeus, c/o Mt. Olympus, applying for a job as a god or goddess. You may write as one of the ones on the chart or become a "new" one. If you become a new god or goddess, choose a quality that you admire or already possess. Decide where you fit on the family tree.

—Write an Acrostic Poem for one of the gods or goddesses.

—Write a ballad or narrative poem about a god or goddess.

ACTIVITY #2

Purpose

To create a new mythological character.

Materials

From the Appendix, you may wish to use some or all of these student pages: Chart of Greek and Roman Mythology, Chart for Colors and Shapes, Chart of Common Symbols, Character Development, and Character Descriptors. You may also wish to use reference books on Mythology.

Preparation

All mythological characters have certain things in common: a position, or job to do; strengths in a particular area; a symbol to represent what the position is. To develop the character's personality, use the Character Development and Character Descriptors Worksheets. Select a position not taken by an already established god or goddess. Try to focus on some of the qualities you admire or possess. Make the character a lot like yourself.

Image

Once the character sketch is completed or nearly completed, autonomously image the character to get a clearer picture of the physical appearance of the character.

Next skim the Chart of Common Symbols and Chart for Colors and Shapes. Again autonomously image the character to design a symbol representative of him/her. Symbols should be simple and direct.

Write

After designing the symbol, write an explanation to accompany it.

ACTIVITY #3

Purpose

To write a myth for the character you've created in ACTIVITY #2.

Preparation

(Do ACTIVITY #2 before continuing.)

Image

(Suggestion to play music during this imagery.) See yourself as the character of mythology that you've created...notice your prefect physical features...and the way you are dressed...feel your power...and wisdom...you are going to begin a journey...through time and space...to a time and place that needs your presence...(longer pause)...decide where you will go...and go there now...if you need to change your appearance, you can do so at will...see yourself at this place...ready to begin your work...observe the people...buildings...plants...the way of life here...go wherever you are needed...see the effect you have on people...look for problems or situations that need your attention...continue this story letting it take you where it will...(pause 3-5 minutes or as music ends)...slowly bring your awareness back to the room as I count to ten...1...2...3...etc.

Write

Use the most interesting idea from your images as the basis for an original myth. Write in the third person.

Follow-Up:

—Use astrology as a basis for a myth.
—Write a myth to explain a specific natural happening (i.e. volcanic eruption).
—Write a myth for specific people (i.e. American Indians).

TALL TALES

A *TALL TALE* is a humorous fantasy story that makes use of exaggeration. The main characters in tall tales have good qualities and motives.

ACTIVITY

Purpose

To explain the origin of a real place using a tall tale.

Materials

Map showing names of towns.

Preparation

Have students each select a city or town with an interesting or unusual name. If time allows, students can write to the Chamber of Commerce c/o that city to get tourist information and historical background. If not, the AAA Tour Guides for states can provide information, too. The intent is to do background research on the geographical area before writing the tall tale since the story will deal with the history of that area—either how it got its name, an exaggerated story about the original founder, or an explanation dealing with natural resources or physical features of the land.

Image

(I suggest that you play music during the imagery.) You are going to go back in time...see yourself leaving the building and approaching the parking lot...in the center is a time machine...the door is open...enter it and close the door securely...notice that the date is of the current year (19   )...set the date for an earlier time...to a time just before the town you selected was founded...feel the rumble and movement of the time machine...feel a sort of dizziness as the machine becomes quiet once again...unlock the door and step out to this new time...observe the sights...and sounds ...of this time...explore the area...look for the person who will make a difference in this place...someone who will change history...someone with good intentions for this place...someone perhaps larger or smaller than life...with special talents or abilities...(longer pause)...when you see this person, notice the manner of dress...and manner of speech...follow this person through an adventure as a sidekick, so that you can tell the story later to the rest of the world...enjoy the adventure...(pause 3-5 minutes)...bring your awareness back to the present time while I count to ten...1...2...3...etc.

Write

Write a tall tale about the story you have imaged. Tell it as if you witnessed the events. Make effective use of exaggeration.

HISTORICAL FICTION

HISTORICAL FICTION uses as its basis, an historical event or specific period in history with fictional characters.

Below are some suggestions for using writing fiction:

—Write a guided fantasy, using an historical event as the theme.

—After imaging a guided fantasy, based upon an historical event, write an eye witness account of it.

—Write the diary for the best friend of, or servant of, or family member of a famous figure in history.

—After researching a particular time period and creating a family tree for an imaginary person, make a family photo album with captions for the major events of that time.

—Create an imaginary character who, in a subtle way, actually changed the course of history but no one ever knew it. Tell his or her story.

—Take a current event and write about it as history.

—Write an interview with an historical figure after or before a major event in history.

—Write the daily horoscope for an important week in the life of someone famous.

—Write a play that focuses on the probable dialogue during an historical event.

SCIENCE FICTION

SCIENCE FICTION is fantasy that is based in unreal places where present human life is not known to survive. Often it is futuristic and includes technical jargon to explain the impossible.

Below are some suggestions for using science fiction:

—Write a guided fantasy about a trip to an unusual place (i.e. underwater, space).

—Write a story about survival on one of the planets.

—Use a superstition as the basis for a science fiction story.

—Write a new episode for Flash Gordon or Buck Rogers.

—Make a tape, complete with sound effects, of a radio broadcast of a U.F.O. visit.

—Make a video tape, narrating the visual scene outside your submarine or spaceship window.

BIOGRAPHICAL FICTION

BIOGRAPHICAL FICTION tells about the life of a real person but individual events and conversations may not always be true. Sometimes the writer eliminates or changes events. Background research often includes interviewing people who know or knew the central figure of the piece.

—After selecting the main character of your story, prepare specific interview questions for people who know or knew him or her. Include their responses.

—After reading a longer biography, write your own, shorter version in a fictional way.

—Write the biography of a famous person, told by one of his or her parents, siblings, or best friends many years later.

—After research into the type of person your character was, tell a story which reflects another side to his or her personality.

147

—Prepare a video of the interviews with people who knew someone famous. Have each tell a personal story remembered about the person.

—Using the Character Development Worksheet, create a profile for a literary character. Use that to write a biography about the character's life in the story.

"All of us collect fortunes when we are children—a fortune of colors, of lights and darkness, of movements, of tensions. Some of us have the fantastic chance to go back to this fortune when grown up."

—Ingmar Bergman

CHAPTER TEN

Non-Fiction

NEWSPAPER NON-FICTION

Try to find as many examples of non-fiction as possible in a newspaper.

FINDING TOPICS

Using a newspaper, magazine, encyclopedia, textbook, or other reference book, write a short non-fiction article.

BRAINSTORMING ARGUMENTS

Using the picture file, list as many possible arguments for the picture that you can (including the absurd). Work in groups. Individuals can select one from the list to elaborate on.

OUTRAGEOUS HOW TO'S

Brainstorm as many "How to _____" topics as you can think of for expository writing. Include "How to Do", "How to Build", as well as "How Not to Do", etc.

NAME THAT TONE

Have students experiment with the effect that the tone has upon a piece of non-fiction writing by reading it aloud to the class. Most arguments use a serious tone; narrative essays are more like conversation and can be humorous or melancholy, casual or thoughtful; reports should be serious and free of colloquialisms. The class can guess the tone after hearing it read. It's also fun to rewrite a piece, changing the tone to see the effect. This is a good lesson since the tone is determined by the author's purpose.

ARGUMENTS

AN ARGUMENT tries to talk the reader into something or move the reader to take action. Although most effective as an oral address, it can also take the form of an editorial, letter, or article. (Arguments make great speeches!)

There are several points to remember when writing an argument:

1. Keep in mind for whom it is intended. This will have a bearing on the tone and vocabulary used.

2. Before writing an argument, write a statement of *purpose* (i.e. I am going to convince my teacher that there should be no final exam.)

3. Next, write a *thesis* or one-sentence summary of the main idea. (i.e. Final exams create so much stress that students cannot demonstrate what they've really learned.)

4. The beginning and ending are the most important parts. They usually state the thesis in broad general terms.

5. The body of the argument contains reasons, explanations, or situations that prove the thesis. Elaborate on each one. Save your best for last.

Here are some suggestions for making the teaching of writing arguments more fun—that's right! Use humor!

—Select a picture from the picture file and use that to get an idea for the topic of the argument (i.e. The spaghetti is talking to the sauce).

—Begin with a lie—something that is definitely not true for the writer, (i.e. I love school, etc.) and prove that it is so with supporting reasons. Save the best reason for last.

—Cluster the topic to be written about to get ideas. From the cluster should come your general statement to begin with and specific ideas to elaborate on. Everything in the cluster need not be used.

—Use a *hot* current topic, either school-related or based on a current event. The topic need not be true, but should cause an emotional reaction and definite opinions. (i.e. Starting tomorrow, pay toilets should be installed in school! or All trading with communist countries should be halted immediately.)

—Take the role of a Fairy Tale *bad guy* and write a letter to Mother Goose convincing her that the story should be rewritten.

—Take the role of a notorious criminal or story villain and write a letter to the one responsible for causing your downfall.

—Write an argument for the best or worst holiday, color, musical style, etc.

—Take the role of a famous author, scientist, or historical figure defending your contribution as the most significant of all time.

—Take your parents' or teachers' side to an argument you've had with them, or advice they've given you. Dramatize the results with another person.

—Use newspapers and magazines to find interesting topics to write about.

—For more serious themes, I suggest that students look at the case to be presented and decide who (what person or groups of persons) would be most affected by the situation. They should then take that person's point of view when writing. It may take some autonomous imaging, but the case usually is argued much more convincingly and realistically.

-NOTES-

IMAGING YOUR ARGUMENT

Purpose

To tune into the tone, vocabulary, target audience, and effectiveness of an argument.

Preparation

The topic and at least a sketchy outline (i.e. notes, cluster) should be done before imaging, or you may wish to use this activity after the writing as preparation for giving a speech.

Image

You are going to be presenting your argument before a live audience...take three slow deep breaths...and close your eyes...before walking to the podium, glance at the note cards in your hands...read your thesis...remind yourself of the supporting statements you'll use to persuade people...(longer pause)...now walk to the podium and look at your audience...you are confident and calm...begin your speech...use a tone that will be effective with this audience...see the understanding and approval on their faces as you persuade them...continue to the end...(pause 2-3 minutes)...restate your conclusions as the audience applauds you...feel the pleasure at a job well done...bring your awareness back to the classroom as I count to ten...1...2...3...etc.

-NOTES-

EXPOSITORY PROSE

The purpose of *EXPOSITORY PROSE* is to inform. These themes may define abstract terms, give instructions on how to do or make something, offer explanations of causes and effects, and present facts and descriptions. For the actual writing, students may wish to use the Connectors Worksheet (See Appendix) to tie thoughts together.

Here are some ideas for writing:

—Cluster abstract nouns (i.e. honesty, faith) and then write.

—Read several poems, articles, song lyrics, etc. with the same theme and then write on the different points of view and interpretations.

—Speak as a famous author would on a topic he's written about. Refer to *your* books, poems, etc. for examples.

—Take one of the *Outrageous How To's* from the warm-up activities and write about it (i.e. How to Ruin a Picnic, How to Cheat on a Test, How to Make a Disgusting Meal, etc.).

—Have the class brainstorm *What Ifs'*. (i.e. What if pigs could fly? What if you could change into something else at will? What if Lady Macbeth had lived today?) Use one as the topic to write about.

—Describe a place after observing it first hand. Tell students to go somewhere (backyard, mall, beach,etc.) and observe while filling in a Multi-sensory Clustering Worksheet. Use that to then write.

—Describe a place in a picture. Again use Multi-sensory Clustering as a prewriting activity.

—Describe a place after hearing a guided fantasy about it. This may be a real or imaginary place in the past, present, or future. Multi-sensory Clustering is a good way to gather ideas before writing.

—Have students select a word card and use free association for 10-15 minutes to gather ideas. Later use this to write the theme.

-NOTES-

BIOGRAPHIES

A BIOGRAPHY is the story of someone's life written by another person. Included are usually the birthdate, birthplace, schooling, significant contributions, and family life.

Included below are some suggestions:

—Using the Character Development Worksheet, interview and fill in information about a classmate or family member. In addition to that information, find out the person's birthday and place of birth. Write a biography of this person's life. (Grandparents and other senior citizens are wonderful subjects.) Photographs may be used as illustrations.

—Using the Character Development Worksheet as a guide, gather information and write a biography about the life of a loved pet.

—Select a contemporary author, scientist, politician, mathematician, or humanitarian that you admire. Gather information from newspapers and magazines before writing your biography. (Sometimes a letter to the person which includes well thought out questions and a self-addressed, stamped envelope will receive a speedy response.)

-NOTES-

AUTOBIOGRAPHIES

An AUTOBIOGRAPHY is a story written by a person about his own life. Not only are facts given, but memories of important events experienced and emotions felt are included. People who had an influence on the writer are also mentioned as well as anything else the writer feels is important.

Suggestions for autobiographies are:

—Using rolls of adding machine paper, make personal time lines. Baby books, family photo albums and interviewing family members will be helpful for filling in the early years. Students should include future hopes and aspirations as well.

—Have students collect photographs that have special meaning to them because of the memories they evoke. Situations may include special pets, teachers, family members, vacations, birthdays, embarrassing moments, homes lived in, deaths that affected them, and moments when there were especially proud. Students may wish to focus the autobiography around one or two of those themes mentioned—writing only about pets and birthdays, for example.

—Select and research someone who made history in some way. Pretend you are that person and tell your own story. (Some students also like to select a character from a novel for this.) I call this activity *The Outrageous Lie* and use an imagery before having students *tell* their life stories to the class, while in costume as this other person.

-NOTES-

THE OUTRAGEOUS LIE

Image

Close your eyes and see yourself becoming the character or person that you have selected to become...as you watch yourself in the mirror, notice that your clothing...and physical features are changing...you are now that other person...speak your new name...hear your new voice...look around at the objects you own and the place where you live...(longer pause)...go back now to your childhood and remember what it was like...(longer pause)...your room...your family...things you did as a child...(longer pause)...moving from your childhood, continue to review the major events of your life...the things that make you feel most proud about yourself...the things that you are most well remembered for...(pause 3-5 minutes)...look into the mirror once again...you will begin to change back as I count to ten...1...2...3...etc.

Write

Write your life story as this famous person or tell your life story to the class. Make sure to dress and speak as this person would. You must convince the audience that you are indeed this other person.

-NOTES-

ESSAYS OF NARRATION

An ESSAY OF NARRATION is an informal essay. It may be a whimsical or humorous treatment of a subject, personal reminiscences, or random observations of life. Its purpose is to interest and entertain.

Suggestions for narrative essays:

—Take any single event from the personalized time line (SEE AUTOBIOGRAPHIES) and write about the experience.

—After observing the participants at an event, (i.e. parade, play, dance, concert) or the activities typical of a particular place (i.e. playground, beach, zoo) write about those observations. Be sure to observe, not participate, to get your perspective for writing.

—Tell about something that you would like to have happen as if it already has (i.e. high school graduation, buying your first car). Begin with the words, *I remember the day...*

—Write about an event that has taken place at school recently.

—Conduct a survey among your peers on a topic of common interest (i.e. learning to drive, blind dates, parents, etc.) and use what you learn to write your own humorous account.

-NOTES-

LITERARY ESSAY & CLUSTERING MODEL

The purpose of a LITERARY ESSAY is to prove something, not to retell the story. It is, therefore, important to be selective in the type of information used.

The essay question can be divided into two basic parts—situation or problem and directives. The situation or problem is usually stated in the first two sentences of the essay question. Have the student take this information and rewrite it in his own words. This becomes the first sentence of the introductory paragraph. Directives are words that tell the student what he needs to do in order to answer the essay question. Some common words used are *choose*, *explain*, *show*, *cite*, *illustrate*, and *tell*.

The LITERARY CLUSTERING MODEL was developed by English teacher, Char Large. It can be used to help the student outline his entire essay in a matter of minutes. Unlike the more traditional method of outlining, this is not only easier and less time consuming, but the student is provided with a visual tool that will keep him organized and on track by simply following the circles and connectors.

Here is a typical essay question and the way it can be set up using the model. The first circle is always the introductory paragraph. The other circles and connectors follow the directives given in the essay question. After the student completes the clustering, he need only to take the information from the circles and establish sentences.

SAMPLE LITERARY ESSAY

People make decisions that can effect someone else. From the stories read this semester, choose two. Choose a character from each work and explain what decision was made. How does this decision effect someone else?

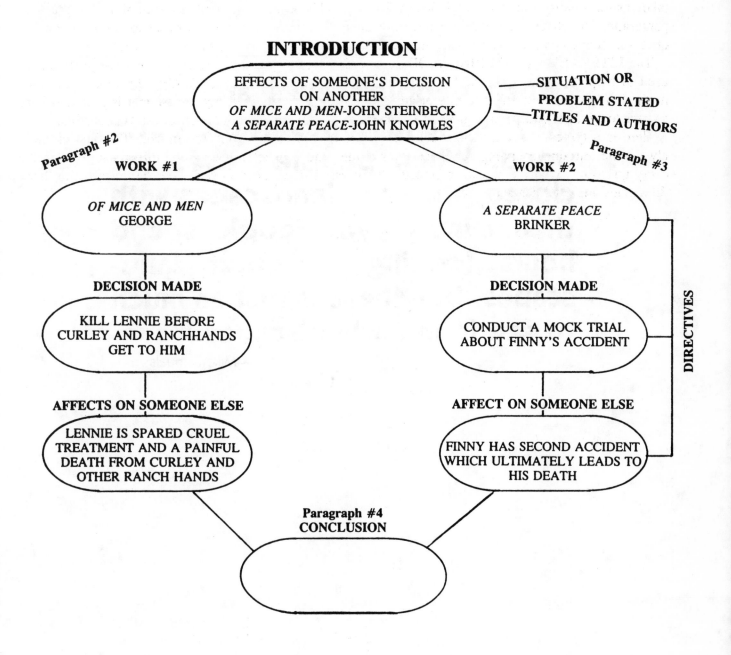

INTRODUCTION

EFFECTS OF SOMEONE'S DECISION ON ANOTHER
OF MICE AND MEN-JOHN STEINBECK
A SEPARATE PEACE-JOHN KNOWLES

SITUATION OR
PROBLEM STATED
TITLES AND AUTHORS

Paragraph #2
WORK #1

OF MICE AND MEN
GEORGE

DECISION MADE

KILL LENNIE BEFORE CURLEY AND RANCHHANDS GET TO HIM

AFFECTS ON SOMEONE ELSE

LENNIE IS SPARED CRUEL TREATMENT AND A PAINFUL DEATH FROM CURLEY AND OTHER RANCH HANDS

Paragraph #3
WORK #2

A SEPARATE PEACE
BRINKER

DECISION MADE

CONDUCT A MOCK TRIAL ABOUT FINNY'S ACCIDENT

AFFECT ON SOMEONE ELSE

FINNY HAS SECOND ACCIDENT WHICH ULTIMATELY LEADS TO HIS DEATH

DIRECTIVES

**Paragraph #4
CONCLUSION**

"When people's eyes are open, they see landscapes in the outer world. When people's eyes are closed, they see landscapes with their mind's eye. People spend hours looking at outer landscapes, but there is just as much to see in inner landscapes."

—Mike Samuels

CHAPTER ELEVEN

Self-Image

WARM-UPS

I CAN'T...BUT I CAN...

Begin a sentence with the words, *I can't* and complete that part with something that you cannot do—either because you don't know how, are not allowed to or are physically unable to. Continue after that with the words, *but I can* and write something that balances or counters the first part. For example, *I can't fly, but I can swim*. Have students write at least ten of these statements.

Some other formulas that can be used in the same way as the above activity are:

I used to be...but now...
I never...but I might...
I always...but I never...
If I could...I would...

ACROSTIC POETRY

Acrostic or name poetry, is simple and fun to write. The name of the person, (or animal, object, story character, place, event, etc.) is written vertically on the left side of the page. Each letter is capitalized and becomes the first letter of the word in that line. The words written should describe the person in a positive way. Each line may be a single word, phrase or a thought that is continued on the next line. Below are some samples:

Joking
Often lazy
Slick
Hates spinach
—Josh Shoenfeld, Gr. 5

Whispers some of her meows
Inquiring
Lazy
Loves to lie by the heater
Oh, that cat is nice!
What will she do next?

—Ronnie Rowe, Gr. 5

For poems about pets, I usually suggest that students image the pet doing something typical for it to do and then try to capture that idea in the poem. Here's a sample:

Rusty-looking
Utterly fabulous senses
Scratching and killing the coon
Tiring from the fight
Yawning and slowly walking home.
—Paul Jeges, Grade 6

161

THE WORKSHOP

If you have not yet done this activity, I suggest that you use it now. It is found in the Introductory Imagery Activities and can be used with many of the journal activities. Students often like to go to their workshops before writing about topics that are very personal to them.

PLAYS ON WORDS

This idea comes from *Dealing With Feelings* (Richards & Standley). Have students write an essay about themselves in a humorous way by first selecting a general category, (i.e. Eggs) and using as many words/phrases associated with it when writing, (i.e. I'm Grade A when..., I had egg on my face..., Some people think I'm cracked when..., If I could break out of my shell....).

THREE BOXES

This activity comes from Dr. Dorothy Sisk. It is so fascinating that I urge you to participate as you read along for the first time. The results reveal much about yourself.

Procedure

At the top of your paper, draw a small box.

Put your pencil down and close your eyes. See a small box in your mind's eye. Look into the box and see what is inside...when you have seen something in the small box, open your eyes.

Write or draw what you saw in the small box near or in the box on your paper. (Wait for all to finish.)

Now pretend that you are indeed the object in the small box. You are going to speak as the object would speak, completing these statements:

I feel...
I must/should...
I need...
Never refer to me as...

Now draw a medium sized box on your paper.

Repeat the same procedure as with the small box. Image to see what is inside and write the four statements, speaking as the object in the medium sized box. (Wait for all to complete this.)

Now draw a large box on your paper. Continue the same as before. (Wait for all to finish.)

Processing Out

The objects in the boxes represent (either symbolically or in actuality) your past values, present state and future dreams. Along with what you have written, the small box reflects the essence of you; the medium box, your day to day life; and the large box, something that you value.

(You may wish to ask students to share one of the boxes that they've written about with the class. Some may also wish to react to the fact that the boxes are representative of themselves.)

Write

Review what you've written for the boxes. Then write what the information means to you or what you may have learned about yourself from it. You may agree or disagree with the theory that the boxes are you.

PERSONAL THOUGHTS

Procedure

Give students a topic and ask them to write, either from personal experience or from a personal point of view on the topic. The writing may be poetry, prose or stream of consciousness. Suggested topics are:

Perfection	Wisdom	Decisions
Imperfection	Yearning	Change
Death	Mental Illness	Power
Birth	Being Handicapped	Pride
Suicide	Abortion	Love
Frustration	Depression	Terminal Illness
Potential	Hunger	Ego
Fear	Challenge	Freedom
Leadership	Anger/Rage	Imprisonment
Loneliness	Empathy	Peace of Mind
Hate		

Students may wish to cluster the word first.

STUDENT SAMPLES

YEARNING

Sitting on the bed,
Tears in my eyes,
Wanting to touch my dreams,
Not succeeding.
—Meredith Glickman, Grade 9

SUICIDE

Giving up to the pressures of today's society
Rejecting the impulse to search for help
Resting peacefully for eternity
Emotionally scarring friends and family forever.
—Kim Tirone, Grade 9

ANSWERS

I guess it helps you when you cry.
But me? I can't do that; I have to live
And love and laugh today, because I know
This joy will not forever stay. And when
Tomorrow's sorrows set in, I will say
That I do not regret these youth-filled times.
And even then my tears will fall so slowly.
And all the carefree thoughts I think today
I will recall with ease and pleasure great.
But you? Because of times that were so bad
You have to cry; you live your life in pain.
To me, it seems you waste a lot of time
At home while crying, missing this life.
    You have forgotten me, your other child.
The one alive and well; you have forgot
That I am still your daughter, not in place
Of sis, but next to her, almost the same
As her, but yet so far from being her.
I wish to love and laugh and live with you.
If you will only let me in your heart.
—Kathleen Brennan, Grade 12

A PIECE OF PAPER

This activity along with the imagery exercise, comes from teacher, Marion McLaughlin.

Preparation

Discuss how the words of a writer tell you something about the writer. This may include the writer's interests, sense of humor or lack of it, background, style, etc.

Image

Sit comfortably and relax...close your eyes...see yourself holding a piece of paper...feel the texture of the paper...feel how thick or thin the paper is...see the color of the paper...notice if the paper has any lines...notice if the paper has any pictures or designs...see if the paper has any writing on it...read any writing that might be on the paper, or image what you might write on it...(longer pause)...think about the author of what was written...crinkle the paper and listen to the sound it makes...look again at the whole piece of paper...now, return to the classroom...when I count to ten, open your eyes...1...2...3...etc.

Write

Write a detailed paragraph describing the paper and what was written on it. Title it, "A Piece of Paper".

SEEING YOURSELF THROUGH SOMEONE ELSE'S EYES

Preparation

Ask students to select a person other than themselves who knows them well. Friends and family members are a good choice.

Image

Close your eyes and see the person that you have selected to describe you...see how the person is dressed...and what the person is doing...watch the person smile when your name is mentioned by someone else...listen as the person talks about you...telling others all about you...the way that person sees you...(longer pause 2-3 minutes)...hear the person tell a favorite story about you...(longer pause)...bring your awareness back to the room as I count to ten...1...2...3...etc.

Write

Speaking as if you are that other person, describe yourself as that person would describe you. Use words and phrases that may be unique to the person speaking. Speak in a conversational tone, as if you (as the other person) are talking to someone else.

166

RECREATE AN ARGUMENT

Procedure

It is always difficult to make dialogue seem natural. Think back to a recent conversation that you've had with someone. Arguments are easiest to recall because with them goes the emotional feelings as well, (remember the ISM discussed in the early chapters of the book?). Try to recreate the argument using only the words that were spoken. Let the reader fill in the gaps as to what is taking place. Don't worry about choppiness.

STUDENT SAMPLE

"Oh, shoot! I think I just went through a red light."

"Yeah you did, and if you do it again you won't be driving at all. I don't ever want to see you speed up to get through a light again!"

(No reply)

"Stop at the Seven-Eleven before we go home."

"Yeah, Dad, okay, you already told me that. You know, the insurance guy told me that it's okay if I drive now."

"No it's not. You don't have insurance."

"Yeah, but he said I'm covered anyway under your policy."

"Well I still want written proof."

"But he said it's okay."

"I don't care!! I said you're not driving alone. Besides, I'm trying to keep the mileage down on the cars."

"Yeah, okay. Hey, I entered another poetry contest, and entered some of my articles from the newspaper in a different one."

"Great, just don't forget to go to the store."

"Yeah, right."

—Kathleen Brennan, Grade 12

WRITING ABOUT THE WEATHER

Procedure

We all are affected by the weather. This activity capitalizes on that assumption and can be done any time of year. I like to do it when there has been a drastic weather change such as: the first day it snows, a sudden thunderstorm, the first warm day, a warm day in the midst of a cold spell, etc.

Simply call everyone's attention to the weather and have them observe it for several minutes. Some may wish to use Multi-sensory Clustering while others will simply *tune in* to what is taking place. Make sure there is enough time to really *feel* what is happening outside.

Suggest that students write about the weather. This may be a descriptive paragraph or focus on how the weather affects them and their inner selves. (Personification, metaphors and similes work well in this writing activity.)

TREE FEELINGS

This activity idea came to me after reading a poem entitled, *Tree Feelings*.

Preparation

Students should select a non-living object for this activity. They will become the object and through imaging, decide whether or not the object likes being what it is.

Image

See yourself becoming the object that you have selected...notice your size...shape...and color...notice where you are and what you are doing here...(longer pause)...think about how it feels to be doing this...examine every aspect of being this object...(longer pause)...decide whether or not you like being this object...bring your awareness back to the room as I count to five...1...2...3...4...5.

Write

Use the following formula:
Title: (object) Feelings
Line #1: I wonder if they like it being   (object)?
Line #2: I suppose they (do/don't)...
Next several lines: Give reasons for what you've said in Line #2.
Skip a line.
Next several lines: Become the object and speak to the reader.
Here are two samples from students who both chose to write about clouds:

CLOUD FEELINGS

I wonder whether they like it being clouds?
I suppose they don't...
They're always being bullied by the wind,
Pushed and shoved in different directions.
Planes have no respect for them
They fly right through the helpless clouds.

It's so cold up here in the sky,
But when I look down on the beaches
I see humans barely clothed
And I am shivering.
—Tom Klein, Grade 9

CLOUD FEELINGS

I wonder if they like it being clouds?
I suppose they do...
It's nothing new.

Yes, 'tis very good to be a cloud
Tee Hee, I'm free
I dance and swirl
And write in white
I can be fat
Or small as a mite
I can be black
Or bring you much bright
I can be white
Or clear out of sight
I can be loving
Gently cooling the air
I can be nothing
It's all in my care

I wonder if they like it being clouds?
I suppose they do not...
It's nothing to want
Clouds sit in the sky
Change colors on high
It must be boring
So boring to be a cloud.
—Michelle Miller, Grade 11

TOP DOG/UNDER DOG

This is another writing activity that comes from Dr. Dorothy Sisk. It uses the fact that we all have conversations with ourselves—usually negative, (I'll never loose weight! I can't do it! I'll probably make a fool of myself!). The dialogue we have with ourselves can have a very real affect upon whether or not we do change or succeed; so why not make it positive rather than negative?

Preparation

Tell students to think of something that they'd really like to change about themselves. It may be physical, such as weight, or an attitude, such as patience. Once that is decided, they should use the formula below and begin to write.

Write

What you will be writing will be a conversation between Top Dog (your positive side) and Under Dog (your negative side). Top Dog will continue to repeat the same statement over and over again until he/she convinces Under Dog to give in. Top Dog's statement begins with the words, *Every day I'm becoming more and more* and is completed with whatever the change is, (patient, self-confident, etc.) The wording may have to be adjusted to fit the words, (Every day I'm loosing more and more weight.) but remains the same throughout. Under Dog will respond each time to Top Dog's statement with perhaps a question, (Oh, yea? What about the chocolate cookies?) or an exclamation, (Sure!) or another statement.

No ditto marks are to be used! You must write out the positive statement each time.

Continue the conversation until Under Dog gets worn down and comes around to the positive way of thinking, if not enthusiastically then subtly. (Usually about ten lines are needed to make the switch.)

-NOTES-

FOUR DOORS

Preparation

Tell students that they will be entering a room with four doors, The Future, The Present, The Past and The Unknown. They may choose any door to enter and later will write about what they found there.

Image

(I suggest that you play music while they image.)

Close your eyes...and get comfortable...listen to your breathing becoming calm...and even...relax...see yourself standing in an empty white room...there is a door directly in front of you...it says The Past on it...read it...examine this door, but do not open it...(longer pause)...now turn and face the next wall...see a door that says, The Present...again look at the door carefully but do not enter...now turn again and see the door marked, The Future...scan this door...but do not enter...lastly look at the fourth and last door...it says, The Unknown on it...examine this door, also...think about what might be behind each of the doors...(longer pause)...decide which door you would like to enter...which world you would like to explore...when you are ready, walk to that door...notice that it is not locked...open the door...smell the air that is coming from the place that you chose...if you have changed your mind, go to another door now...if not, step through this door...you are in control of this journey...you may go anywhere...and do anything that you really want to do...enjoy this adventure for the next five minutes of clock time which is a long enough time to do all of the things that you want to do...(pause five minutes or near to the end of the music playing)...the time has come to return to the classroom...as I count to ten, bring your awareness back to this room...1...2...3...4...etc.

Write

Before writing, students may wish to share their experience. Ask if anyone does. Then tell students to write about what was found behind the door chosen. This may sound like a dream experience, a story or even a factual account.

Variation

Later you may wish to have students return to this room for a specific purpose, such as going back in time to a particular historical event or into the future to look at some new technology. The door to the present could represent a conflict to be solved in their day-to-day lives.

IMAGING GOALS

Preparation

Ask students to think about a specific goal that they have for themselves. It may be personal or professional but must be a goal that can be achieved, either by saving money, working hard, going to school, etc. (Introduce the Workshop activity prior to this.)

Image

You will be going to your workshop to image this goal and all of its aspects . . . close your eyes and go now to your workshop . . . as you look around your workshop, change anything that you feel you need to change at this time . . . (longer pause) . . . sit in front of the viewing screen . . . turn the controls to Goal-viewing . . . see yourself on the screen . . . you have already accomplished the goal . . . listen as you say that you have accomplished the goal . . . notice the smile of pride on your face . . . see where you are . . . and what you are doing . . . examine every aspect of this goal . . . the place . . . the time . . . people who might be sharing this moment with you . . . (longer pause) . . . look for some of the reasons that you have been successful with this goal . . . any special efforts . . . or training that you've engaged in . . . (longer pause . . .)hear yourself once again saying that you have achieved the goal . . . feel the pride . . . feel a power stronger than yourself, outside of yourself . . . in the cosmos . . . that has been with you all of the way . . . and is still now . . . know that you can reach this goal . . . as you dim the screen . . . think of the different aspects of the goal . . . and how it can be achieved . . . keep these ideas with you as I count to ten . . . 1 . . . 2 . . . 3 . . . etc.

Write

Actually what you will be doing is making a montage or Map of the goal in its final stage—completed. Included should be the following things (either using pictures, words, symbols, objects or a combination of all of them):

1. You having completed the goal, (i.e. a visual representation of yourself).
2. Affirmations/statements that say that you *have* completed what you set out to do. Be specific, (i.e. Here I am, ten pounds thinner. I feel great. I look great. I knew I could do it!)
3. All aspects of the goal, (i.e. ticket stubs and map if the goal was a trip, scorecard and tees if the goal was your golf score).
4. A symbol that represents a power outside of your own human power. We all have that strength to draw upon. It may, but does not have to be a religious symbol. The Chart of Symbols in the Appendix may be helpful.
5. Other people involved with the achievement of the goal.

NOTE: Place your imaged goal in a place where you can see it. It is a positive reinforcement as well as a reminder. It is not, however, cast in stone. Before you reach this goal, you may wish to modify it sightly or change it all together. That's good, too. It shows that you are growing and not afraid to change your goals as you do.

Some people even find that once they have imaged the goal it will become a reality without ever making the Map. They believe that if you can *see* it, then you can *be* it! (I'm one of those people.)

JOURNALS

Many of the activities in the rest of the book as well as all of the ones in this section on SELF-IMAGE make excellent journal entries. There are many ways to use journals, from a daily classroom writing experience based upon the content of the day's lesson to a private activity done at home. However used, journals are the most *therapeutic* type of writing since they often contain the author's innermost thoughts, feelings and reactions to the writing stimulus. For this reason respecting the privacy of the author is of the utmost importance. Below are some suggestions for journal-keeping:

Tell students that you will not read their journals. Many students will, from time to time, want to share aloud or ask you to read what they've written. I often ask if there is anyone who would like to share anything with me (privately), with a friend or with the rest of the class; but the purpose is not for sharing as with other writing that you will do. One way to know if the students want it read is to ask them to place a marker in the page and hand it in. Another is to have them only write on the left page for their entries. The right sides remain blank unless they put a note there asking you to read the entry. You can also write any comments that you have on the right side.

Do not correct journals. When you do read the entries, do not look for grammatical mistakes. If you must check to see that students are writing each day, ask that they date entries at the top of the page. You can then place a check (or better yet a smile face) next to the date without reading what was written. Keep your comments personal, (a simple *"I know what you mean"*) and nonjudgemental.

Expect to be shocked. Once in a while a student will deliberately try to test you by writing in large letters, writing obscenities or writing about you. If it doesn't end after a couple of days, there is nothing wrong with writing a comment about the purpose of the journal, the benefits of the journal or how *you* feel about their comments. This usually ends it.

At first, have a set time for journal-keeping. You know that in order for something to become a habit, it must be practiced. Some teachers use the journal during the first or last ten minutes of class. Some prefer to set aside one day a week for it. Others may ask students to react in writing at home when they have time to think. Even if you cannot stick to a schedule for more than a month at a time, try for that long at least.

Encourage independent journal-keeping. Journals are a wonderful way to release energy without anyone getting hurt. Encourage students to use their journals to get out anger and frustration; to think aloud about problems that are bothering them; to tell someone something that the cannot tell them in person; to keep track of events and emotions during special times in their lives such as moving away, trying out for the school play or sports team, graduation, etc.

Journal Topics to Begin With:
—Describe a scene from top to bottom, front to back or left to right.
—Describe yourself from top to bottom, front to back or inside to outside.
—Write a letter to someone.
—Write a love poem to someone.
—Write a plan for a telephone conversation you might have in the future, (i.e. job interview, complaint about a product, etc.)
—Draw a picture of your thoughts.
—Draw a picture of yourself ten years from now.
—Listen to music and write about the way it makes you feel.
—Write about what you saw during a guided fantasy.

—Write a guided fantasy of your own.
—Draw a cartoon of yourself.
—Make a list of things you like to do. Circle your favorite one and image it.
—Doodle to create a design.

WANTED POSTERS

Procedure

Select a person for whom you will make a wanted poster. (You may choose yourself.) Take a photograph or draw a picture of the person for the poster. Make a list of that person's positive personality traits, talents, hobbies, etc. Use this list to write a humorous description to go with the picture on the Wanted Poster. You must decide what the person is wanted for, (i.e. Wanted for Making People Laugh), include a physical description and possible *hangouts* and associates, and determine a reward to be given if brought in.

Variations

Pets, fictional characters and famous people are good subjects for Wanted Posters, too. Objects of value only to the person owning it (i.e. a lucky hat) or goals (i.e. an *A* on the final exam) can make interesting topics.

ADVERTISEMENTS

Procedure

This is similar to the Wanted Poster activity. The idea is to write an advertisement for yourself or something else. When people are the subjects, focus on the positive only. Sometimes it's fun to list the ads anonymously and ask members of the class to guess who the person is or who sounds the most interesting to them from what the ads say.

Variation

Bring in some objects that students are unfamiliar with. Tell them to pretend that they just found one of the things in the attic and should write an ad to sell it. Even though they do not know what it is, they should try to pretend that they do and write a most interesting ad for it.

OUTRAGEOUS RESUME

Procedure

Pretend you are a non-living thing and write a letter of application for a job that you'd like to have. You may wish to have the job of Mrs. So-and-so's red marking pen, Jack in the Beanstalk's ax or the red phone in the oval office.

SUGGESTED FORMULAS FOR WRITING ABOUT YOURSELF & OTHERS

SOMEDAY...

Begin each line with the word *Someday* . . . and complete it with a wish that you have. Make the first two or three say something about your every day wishes and slowly move away from yourself to the world in general. End the writing with the word *Someday* . . . .

ONE WINDOW IS ALL I NEED...

Begin your poem or essay with the line, *One window is all I need*, and continue to write about this imaginary window in a personal way. For example:

One window is all I need
To revolve in and out of myself
To pass through adventures
With people and life
To return to myself
And grow.
—K.K. Hess

THE IMPORTANT THING ABOUT...

This formula is great to use when writing about another person. I've also used it to write about holidays, (i.e. Thanksgiving), abstract concepts, (i.e. Democracy, Faith, etc.), book characters, and famous people and events. It can even serve as an outline for a longer essay.

Line #1: The important thing about __(name)__ is __(most striking attribute.)__
Line #2: He/she is also _____
                       _____
                       _____   (list other attributes)
                       _____
      and   _____
Last Line: But the most important thing about __(name)__ is
__(repeat what was said in line #1 or say the same thing in another way.)__

Keep the focus positive when writing about people you know.

CAPTURING THE MOMENT

This formula freezes an instant and examines various aspects of it.

Line #1: Adverb or Adjective   Asleep
Line #2: I was _____   I was dreaming
Line #3: Verb or Adjective   Content

Line #4: I am _____   I am not alone
Line #5: Verb or Adjective   Comforted
Line #6: I will _____   I will try again
Line #7: Verb or Adjective   Refreshed
Line #8: Now _____   Now I can.

EMOTIONS & ACTIONS

Line #1: Write three *ing* words   Examing, studying, testing,
Line #2: I am _____   I am searching for a cure
Line #3: Write three adjectives   Tired, tense, drained
LINE #4: I feel . _____   I feel so close...

* * * *

Line #1: What if _____
Line #2: I Might _____
(leave a space between lines 2 & 3)
Line #3: What if _____
Line #4: I could _____
(leave a space between lines 4 & 5)
Line #5: What if _____
Line #6: I would _____
(leave a space between lines 6 & 7)
Line #7: Ask a question.

* * * *

Line #1: When I _____ (describe action)
Line #2: _____(describe where action takes place)
Line #3: Write 2 of 3 words that describe how you feel
Line #4: I wish I could _____(describe action)
Line #5: Tell reason why

* * * *

Title: EMOTION
Line #1: I _____ (describe what you did to show how you were feeling)
Line #2: Write 3 words that describe how you felt
Line #3: Make a statement or ask a question with regard to what is written in the first two lines

* * * *

Title: A WORD ENDING IN *ING*
Line #1: I am _____ (describe where you are)
Line #2: Write a simile telling how you feel
Line #3: I would like _____
Line #4: Write a statement that describes a detail of something that is happening around you while you are feeling this way. This should be something removed from your immediate situation. (i.e. *A bird's cry can be heard in the distance, or Children finish the tower of their sand castle, or A crab darts along the waters edge.*)

Line #1: If I had _____

Line #2: I'd feel _____

Line #3: I would _____

Line #4: I wouldn't _____

Line #5: Fortunately _____

Line #6: Unfortunately _____

* * * *

Line #1: If I could be _____

Line #2: I'd _____ (describe what you'd do)

Line #3: _____ (describe how you'd do it)

Line #4: _____ (describe where you'd do it)

Line #5: Exclamation that shows how you'd feel

SUGGESTED TOPICS FOR WRITING ABOUT YOUR-SELF

These topics may be used for both poetry and prose, both fiction and non-fiction.

—Things That I Don't Understand (About School, Parents, Drugs, Competition, Other Kids, Space, The World, etc.)

—My Hopes for the Future

—My Favorite Place To Be

—The Best Vacation

—A Best Friend

—A Perfect Room

—A Person Who Has Influenced My Life

—My Earliest Memory (Family photo albums can give you ideas.)

—My Pet

—The Worst Day of My Life

—My Most Embarrassing Moment

—My Proudest Moment

—The Day I Met . . .

—My Favorite T.V. Show (or Movie, Book, Play, Singing Group/Band, Musical Style, Book Character, Hero, Villain, etc.)

—How to Be a Hero

—How Not to be a Hero

—My Parents Really Aren't So Bad (or Brother, Sister, etc.)

—Fortunately/Unfortunately (Tell a story, real or fantasy, beginning each new event with the words *fortunately* or *unfortunately*. Continue to flip-flop back and forth between them.)

—How I'll Make My Dreams Come True

—A Hunch That Paid Off

—My Greatest Challenge

—I Didn't Do It

—I Couldn't Do It

—But *Everyone* Is Doing It!

—My Outer Self

—My Inner Self

—If I Had a Million Dollars To Give Away

—If I Could Have One Wish For The World

—If I Could Be Anyone Else but Me

—The Real Me

—Things I Do That I Don't Understand

—My Roots

—A Daydream

—A Dream

—What I Think About When I Don't Think About Anything

—I Am Really Descended From Royalty

—Who Am I?

—My Epitaph (or the epitaph of an ancestor)
—My Ancestors' Arrival in this Country
—Things I'd Like to Tell My Ancestors
—Things I'd Like to Tell My Grandchildren
—My Family Tree
—My Worst Argument
—If I Could Be Completely Honest With . . ., Here's What I'd Say
—My Home Remedy For . . .(Getting Rid of Warts, etc.)
—If My Pet Could Talk
—If I Had Wings
—If I Could Grant Three Wishes To Someone
—If I Could Go Back (or Ahead) In Time...
—A Spell I'd Like To Cast

The spoken or the written word
Should be as clean as is a bone,
As clear as is the light,
As firm as is a stone.
Two words will never serve
As well as one alone.

—Anonymous

CHAPTER TWELVE

Finishing Touches

POLISH TO PUBLISH

I prefer to use the word, polish, rather than edit, since polishing implies that what you have is already good. (You wouldn't polish a rotten apple, now would you?) The suggestions given are general rules that I follow with most writing. There are also many other things that you can do during this last stage of writing that are more specific to the age level, ability level, specific type of writing piece done and individual student styles. I leave those to you, the teacher, for you know your own students' capabilities.

Polishing suggestions are divided into two sections: Polishing the Writing and Polishing the Presentation of the Writing. The first deals with ways to make the words flow and the meaning come through more clearly. The second part gives some ideas for making the writing piece visually attractive. This is just as important, since it is the visual layout of writing that first gets your attention. As you will see, you don't have to be an artist to make it look pleasing to the eye.

Grading is always a *hot* issue when it comes to creative expression and how you approach it can kill or encourage students' desire to write. There is a list of ways to approach grading of creative writing which may be useful when the time comes to make that decision. (There are also some ideas to save you some of the reading and rereading of student work during the polishing process.)

The last step in the writing process is the sharing of the writing. Not all writing is meant to be shared, (i.e. journals, writing that just didn't *work* for the writer) but much of it is. There are many ways to publish student work. Acceptance builds confidence so I encourage as much sharing as possible on the classroom level. Next comes displaying work for other classes to see, school publications and submissions to literary magazines. I've tried to include suggestions for each of these types of publishing.

Above all, I feel that writing should be taught as a process. So often students feel that they are *done* and then must go back and rewrite the same thing. This makes them angry. If, however, they know from the start that this is just the first step, (I usually say, "Right now you're just a writer—not an editor or a publisher. Don't worry about anything except writing right now,") and not the entire process, they don't think of it as *done* until it's been published. This also means that you, as the teacher, must allow time for the polishing and publishing stages as well. It can't always be done *tonight for homework*. Thinking and mulling time are very important steps in the process, too.

POLISHING THE WRITING

GENERAL GUIDELINES FOR TEACHERS

—Many of the activities in the chapter on STYLE can be used to polish writing. As you listen to or read student work, try to suggest the use of similes, metaphors, alliteration or parallel form when appropriate. Without getting specific, your comment might be with regard to a need for rhythm or a need for a more unique description. Let the students experiment and choose what works best for them.

　　—If you find that word or phrase has been overused, simply circle it throughout the composition. Then write a question, such as, "Did you want to emphasize this? If not, substitute similar words or phrases,"

　　—If the writing does not seem to *do* anything because of the way it's written or because of trite words and phrases, brainstorm other words with the student and the rest of the class for better, more vivid ways to describe action and characters. Let the student then take the list and select from that.

　　—I begin much of what I have to say about a student's writing with the words, "I noticed that you have..," This way I am not judging what was written but commenting on it. It takes some of the sting out of getting feedback from the teacher.

　　—My first comments are always positive. There is always something positive that you can say about the creative efforts of another person! When I do make a suggestion I try to give it energy by getting excited at the prospect of making it even better. ("That was really nice. Thank you for sharing it. I'll bet it would sound neat with some alliteration in the beginning part. Yes, yes. That's the place. What do you think?")

　　— React to writing in a personal way first. Then as a teacher. ("I love the way you read it. I knew just how you felt when you read the part about...My dog used to do the same thing! Wow! That was a really beautiful idea. You really captured your own sense of humor in that. Thanks!)

　　— The ending is just as important as the beginning. Suggest to students some of the following ways that they can come full circle with their writing: End by saying the same thing as the title in either a sentence, phrase or exclamation.

　　End with a summary statement that *says it all*.

　　End with saying the same thing that was said in the first line, but use a different way to say it.

　　End with a broad statement or question about life in general as it relates to the theme.

　　Here is a student sample that demonstrates effective use of the last lines. The picture that sparked the writing was one of a sewing machine. Jenny's first title was *Sewing* but she later changed it to *The Mender* when she ended it the way she did.

STUDENT SAMPLE

The Mender

Sleek, technological, impersonal
Straining to mend
Giving her a feeling of control
Sewing things back together
If only she could do it with her life...
the easy way.
　　—Jennifer E. Feldman, Gr. 12

—Sometimes your suggestions for a piece will come from an intuitive feeling about the rhythm or rhyme. Here is a sample poem that I felt needed a last rhyming line at the end and suggested one or two to the student. Cover the last line and read it. Decide for yourself, as the student had to, whether it needs the added last line.

STUDENT SAMPLE

Bookworm

Have you noticed lately my dear,
the holes that seem to appear
in all of the books on my top shelf?
I think there is a bookworm
feasting through the pages
with wire framed glasses
and a red bow tie he's had for ages.
He's really quite knowledgeable, my dear.
He reads 3,000 books each year
Then when he's done
Here comes some fun.
He sits down and feasts,
And grins ear to ear.
    Deborah Harwood, Grade 10

—If students seem to be telling more than is needed, ask these questions:
Does every word in the sentence contribute to the central theme?
Does every sentence contribute to the central theme?
Is there a better way of saying this?
Is the language explanatory...or evocative? Cut out as much of the explanatory as you can. Strengthen the evocative language with metaphors, language rhythms and a unifying thread. Describe images!
—Punctuation and spelling should be the final step of the polishing, although corrections may have been made in these areas along the way. Suggest that students read each others' papers to find errors. As a final check for spelling, have them read the theme *backwards*. This way they see each individual word and not groups of words and phrases.
—A good editing practice is to transpose prose to poetry. This helps students to see that the words they keep are very important. It reinforces the idea that cutting out words can make it better.
—Unity comes by doing two things: coming full circle and having a unifying thread. Some ways to be sure of having a unifying thread is through the use of recurrences, (recurring words, sounds, images and feelings). Both fiction and non-fiction must have this to be effective. This is what gives the piece power; not just the repetition of a word but the flow of the key idea throughout.
In this sample, the student's key idea runs throughout. Notice the types of recurrences used, the parallel forms and the effective use of opposite desires.

Desire
Seeing a long untraveled road on a peaceful day from within the confines of a locked room, aching to feel the road underneath my feet, to see everything it passes through, to do cartwheels and jumps down the road, not wasting time. The road is open, inviting me to experience it, to revel in it. I want to run laughing and singing down the road; but I can't break the window.

Sweet slumber, take me away. Fill me with your deep dark warmth. Breathe in me. Let my eyes grow heavy and close out the world. Bring me meandering through the spirit, carefree and unburdened for a few short hours.

Sweet, sweet slumber, take me away....

—Jennifer E. Feldman, Grade 12

—Encourage oral reading. It causes students to hear the rhythm and flow of the writing better than any other technique can. It also gives students an audience to communicate their ideas to and a support group which can offer ideas and suggestions when called upon to do so. One teacher suggests having the student read and then ask the audience, *What would you like to hear more about?* This is a positive way to open up the discussion and clarify the written words.

—To make reading easier, I suggest that students write on every other line of the paper. This extra space can be used by student and teacher alike when changing and rearranging words during the polishing.

—Introduce editing marks to the class and in groups. Have them review compositions of the members together. (Writing on ditto masters makes duplication quick and easy.) Since it is a group effort, the drudgery is eliminated and they also learn to use the same editing language.

—Talking and sharing in two's before reading aloud to the class is an excellent way to give students the confidence and positive feedback that they may need and helps them to clarify ideas while they are still fresh in their minds.

—Oral reading can be done at home by either reading to someone else or reading aloud into a tape recorder and playing it back. *THERE IS NO SUBSTITUTION FOR ORAL EDITING.*

—Give students suggestions on *how* to improve their writing not *what* to say. Let them have the final say after hearing the opinions of others. It has to be right for them.

—If something is not working for a student, let him *trash it* and begin again. It is not worth the energy and frustration, not to mention the time spent. Every piece of writing doesn't have to go through the entire polishing process. Sometimes I suggest writing three poems and select only the best to polish and publish. Let's face it-that's how it happens in the real world anyway.

—Remind yourself and the students that the process is more important than the product. All writers have bad days. All writers have one phase or another of the process that they prefer over the rest. Share some of your own experiences and feelings about this with them.

—Encourage their rewriting attempts. Make them feel that they *can* make it better just by changing a word here or a sentence there. ("Yes! That does sound better. That was a good idea.")

—Do move about the room during the writing and rewriting phases. Read, listen, question, admire and encourage. Be genuinely interested in each individual's style and ideas. Try to bring out uniqueness rather than conformity to one style.

—Divide the class into writing teams from time to time. One student is the writer, another the illustrator, another the editor and finally the publisher who shares the work with an audience. Team writing gives everyone a break during the process. At first let them select the job they are best at; later switch so all get the experience at each.

GENERAL GUIDELINES FOR STUDENTS

—Repetition of a word should be done to create emphasis. Otherwise try using a synonym or a more specific word, (i.e. dog-hound-basset hound) to clarify the image. This usually happens with nouns.

—Using action verbs can make the images come alive. (Try taking a piece without action verbs and transpose it. You'll be amazed.)

—The number of adjectives and adverbs is not as important as which ones are used. Make the words create a vivid image.

—If something has been said that way a million times, say it in a new or surprising way.

—Switching the order of words in a sentence can make it sound better. Write the sentence parts on separate slips of paper and rearrange until you like the sound of it. This can also be done with the lines of a poem.

—Oral reading is the best way to find things that prevent the flow of ideas. Read aloud to a friend or to a group. You will pick up things like incorrect verb forms and word usage. Members of the group can also ask you to clarify something you've read. Through your explanation you will find a better way to convey the meaning. The group may also be able to help you to find just the right way of saying something. Brainstorm with them for ideas.

—Don't try to do everything at once. Work on a piece. Put it away. Work on it again. The time you spend between working on the writing and polishing it can be very important. You need time to get away from it so you can come back to it with a fresh perspective.

—As you read over your writing, experiment with describing things using similes and/or metaphors.

—If you want to establish a more even rhythm, try using alliteration, parallel form or repetition of a key word, phrase, or idea.

—Everything you write is not going to work for you. If you've tried everything suggested and it still lacks that *something*, allow yourself to get rid of it and move on to something else. A fresh idea may be just the thing to get you out of your slump.

—Some of your best ideas for writing style will come from reading and listening to others read aloud. Always be thinking about how you can make someone's good idea work for you, too.

—Read a variety of writing styles. Find a couple of authors that you'd feel comfortable using as models for your own writing and see what seems to work for them. Try writing something similar or writing in a similar way.

GUIDELINES FOR POETRY

—Poems create reality. They don't explain it. Let the reader find his own explanation. Let the writing speak for itself.

—The line of the poem is what gives it structure. It may be determined by: a breath stop (natural pause), emphasis (isolating a word or phrase), ideas (one image per line), the tempo or rhythm of the words, rhyme, a need to create interest or suspense for visual effect (concrete poetry).

—The source of a poem should be a sensory image, not an idea. Ideas should be presented through the images associated with it.

—Emotions should be felt by the reader through the descriptions of the images rather than stated in the poem. (Don't say that she is sad; tell the reader that she is crying.)

—Concrete images rather than generalities work best to create interest.

—Poems do not have to depend upon logic to get from one line to the next or from the beginning to the end. They do depend upon intuitive connections between disparate things.

—Similes and metaphors can create links between disparate things. Relationships of this kind give energy to the poem and spark the imagination.

—Using rhyme limits vocabulary used. Write the poem first, then decide whether to rewrite it with rhyme. The same is true of rhythm. Write first, then read *aloud* to determine the flow and the rhythm.

—Real experiences can make the best topics. Even an imaged experience becomes a real experience when vivid. Dreams, daydreams and thoughts can be the heart of a poem.

—Since a poem is the words of the writer it should use speech that is natural for the writer. Use a dictionary or thesaurus only to avoid sounding trite or repetitive.

—Always read poems aloud. Use a voice that fits the mood created by the poem.

GUIDELINES FOR PLAYS

—Tell the story through speech and actions rather than descriptions. Try to avoid using a narrator.

—Stage directions are useful, but don't overdo them. Leave several blank lines between speaking parts when writing the play. Later through imaging the actions, walking through the play and seeing the area where the play will be performed, you can add appropriate stage directions.

—Avoid having too many characters. Try to limit the number of actors to no more than five or six. This will also make casting easier.

—Avoid elaborate settings and special effects. In the theater this will not be easy to do. Keep in mind as you write, how this will be seen by the audience. Try to make the most of simple props and setting changes.

—Use a printed playscript as a model, to see the way to put things together on the page.

—Write your play on a ditto master when working in a group. This will make immediate duplication easy and facilitate editing and rehearsal.

—When performing plays try to use language and gestures that are typical for the characters. Make it sound like everyday speech—conversation. This means that incomplete sentences, dialects and colloquialisms are acceptable. They may even enhance the performance.

—To create believable dialogue, ad lib with a partner while a tape recorder is taping you. This will help you to get the dialogue to flow.

—One-man shows are most effective if the actor *becomes* the character and then speaks rather than memorizing the speech. If the actor has a firm understanding of the character and the situation, the words will flow naturally.

POLISHING THE PRESENTATION

—Write using special lettering such as calligraphy.

—Write or type onto colored paper.

—Use computer graphics to put a border around the paper.

—Use a simple repeated pattern (i.e. star, hexagon, etc.) to create a border around the paper.

—Paint a watercolor scene. When the paper dries, write on the painting using pen and ink.

—Cut out a cartoon, newspaper or magazine picture and glue onto construction paper. Type your poem on white paper and cut to size that will also fit on the construction paper.

—Make a mobile. Each line of the poem can be written on a separate hanging shape. Shapes used should reflect the theme. Hang one under the other so it can be read in the correct order. This works very well for acrostic poems.

—Mount a photo of the person or pet written about next to the writing.

—Set up a scene or situation to photograph and use that with the writing.

—Trace a picture or cartoon.

—Mount objects that are mentioned in the writing around the words. Small flat objects such as tickets, keys, safety pins, pressed flowers, coins, etc. work well.

—Draw a simple line drawing of one thing mentioned. This can be a hat, door, traced hand, or shapes that suggest an object.

—Draw a cartoon character. Keep it simple. The body can be an object, such as a pencil, bottle or cloud or a blob with arms and legs. Some cartoon characters don't have hands or feet. Look at the comics to get some ideas.

—Make a fancy capital letter for the first word's first letter or for the words in the title. If the writing is about an animal, make the letter look like it has fur, etc.

—Use colored pens and markers for color words or phrases that show different emotions. A poem about water could be written in blue. A poem about snow could be written in chalk on black paper. Make the color work for you. Use color to emphasize one word throughout, writing the rest in another color.

—Use computer graphics or coloring book illustrations to find appropriate pictures for illustrations.

IDEAS ON GRADING

Brief is best. Save yourself and the students some time by making the length of the assignments minimal most of the time. Have them write only the beginning or ending of the story, one scene, one dialogue, etc. It will take you less time to read and the students less time to recopy after polishing.

As an incentive, you may wish to require only one part of the story to be written for a *B* grade but the entire story for an *A*.

Give no grade before it's time. Rather than allowing students to settle for a low grade, give *no* grade until it has been completed, (edited and recopied). The choice is then to receive a *B* if it is good, and *A* if it is very well done and a zero for not having finished it.

To facilitate this concept, set up a time line and simply put a check in the grade book as each step is completed. This way you do not have to grade and re-grade along the way.

Grade the content after listening. Sometimes it's difficult to be objective about the content when you are looking at red marks all over the paper for the mechanics. Grade the student after hearing him/her read the poem, story or essay. Then collect the papers and give a second grade for mechanics. This will save you time because you'll have the first grade in the book before you even begin. It also encourages students to prepare to read orally, and make many of the corrections that might be overlooked without oral reading.

Don't grade everything. School should be a place where students can fail safely. If there is always the threat of a grade, they will never take risks. Give them the opportunity to try new things and select the one that worked best to be handed in for a grade.

My rule is that they *must* try every activity. Then they can decide whether or not to go back and rework it or try a different approach to it. They might write five Haiku poems before deciding on one that sounds good. The extra practice is much better than doing it once, failing, loosing self-confidence and turning off to writing.

Predetermine the number of writings required for a grade of *B* and a grade of *A*. Students can then select what they feel are their best works and submit them. Make a provision that mechanical errors may effect the overall grade but the content of the writing will not be judged.

Since you will determine how many are required and what types of writing will be done, there is not much of a chance that a student can earn an undeserved grade. You may require a poem that uses metaphors, a narrative essay which follows your guidelines, four descriptive paragraphs that use sensory images to describe characters and setting and one optional writing piece of their choice. Keeping a writing folder for all of the writing done can serve as a bank when putting together an anthology of writings.

Skim the papers for common mistakes. Jot down examples on an overhead transparency, rather than making marks on the students' papers. The next day in class, present all of the mistakes to all of the students for discussion. Then return the papers and see if students can find any errors before writing the final draft. The transparency can be left on the screen while they reread their compositions. Make it a fun activity—laugh at all of the crazy mistakes without making it personal.

Let them search for the mistakes. There are several ways to edit writing other than the teacher's reading every word on every paper and marking it. Here are a couple that work well:

Students work in pairs or small groups to do the editing together.

Return a checklist with a tally only of the grammatical errors, (i.e. spelling—5, verb tense—2, etc.) and see if the student can find his own mistakes. You simply put a check in your grade book that it was handed in on time.

Students write sample essays, etc. with mistakes in them. They then exchange papers. Their grades will be the final draft of the papers they now have.

Have students work in teams to write and edit work. I like to pair a highly creative student with a highly logical one. The result is that they both learn the other's skill while writing together. They both get the same grade.

Don't grade every skill every time. If you have just taught metaphors, then only grade on the ability to use metaphors this time. Once a student has mastered a skill, check it off on a list similar to the one provided in the Appendix, (Writing Skills Checklist). The final grade at the end of the unit can be based upon the number of areas where mastery has been demonstrated.

Grade only on content. Even though correct spelling and punctuation may be a requirement on the final draft, it does not have to receive a grade. Grade the content on such things as clarity, organization and completeness. The mechanics do not add to or detract from the grade—they just get taken care of.

On longer pieces, you may even point out the mistakes and conference with the student about them rather than asking for another draft. ("How could you have said this better? If you were to write this over, what would you say?") After all, isn't the content the *most* important aspect?

Ask for a volunteer to have his/her paper used as a sample in finding mistakes. To take the displeasure out of it, remind them that everyone else will have to do their own polishing while the volunteer gets his/hers done for *free* during class.

Tape your suggestions. Have each student hand in a blank tape with a longer writing piece. You tape your reactions and suggestions rather than marking the paper. Return the tape and the paper to the student. It's a good way to encourage the student, make personal comments without fear of embarrassment and say what you would like to say without writing it all down on the paper. Students really look forward to the comments on tape, and the same tape can be a way of reviewing comments on previous writing to see growth.

Collect writing over time and grade only on the progress made. Begin with a sample short story before instruction. Then add to the folder as you cover the various aspects of a short story. Finally write another story and compare the two. Students will marvel at the progress they have made and the better writers now are forced to compete with themselves and not the rest of the class. A good writer who experiences no growth really doesn't deserve an *A* as much as a poor writer who has made excellent progress. What you are really striving for is self-evaluation.

PUBLISHING IDEAS

Publishing means sharing work with an audience. It includes displays on the walls and bulletin boards, class and school literary magazines and newspapers and submissions to national magazines. It can also include letters to the editor of local newspapers, school assemblies for reading and acting out original plays and community displays in storefronts and local libraries. The list below should give you plenty of ideas to get you started.

Publish in the P.T.A. bulletin.
Publish in a community flyer/newsletter.
Decorate the school buses.
Have a Writing Fair or a Poetry Day, etc.
Decorate school halls, doors, ceilings, windows, etc.
Make posters or billboards.
Create a photo essay.
Put it on a flag or bumper sticker.
Make a radio play recording.
Share it with senior citizens or hospital patients.
Send it to a writer that you admire.
Decorate a jar or paperweight with it.
Frame it.
Make a wall-sized mural.
Attach it to a helium balloon and release it.
Mount or stitch it onto a banner.
Etch it, carve it, decoupage it, or bake it in a fortune cookie.
Hang it on a tree (Poet Tree).
Send it to the Board of Education, Principal, Mayor, President, etc.
Decorate a tee shirt.
Give it to someone as a gift.
Put it to music.
Create a dance to tell the story.
Put it on a kite.
Translate it into different languages. (Don't forget shorthand!)
Paint it on the sidewalk or pavement.
Create a comic strip.
Write a public service announcement. Make it into a video.
Pantomime it.
Make it into a filmstrip. This can be done using 35mm film and turning the camera on its side to take all of the shots. When you get it developed, ask that they do not cut the negatives apart to make slides but just develop the film. It will fit into standard filmstrip projectors.
Make a slide series with tape to narrate it.

MAGAZINES THAT PUBLISH STUDENT WORK

There will come a time when you feel you'd like to submit a piece of writing to a national magazine for publication. Below is a list of magazines who often use student writing. The ones with the * after them are more for older students while the others may publish a story or poem written by and for younger children. They also publish original artwork.

Whether you do or do not submit anything, here are good writing activities to try with your students:

Divide the class so that each student has the name of a magazine and its address. Have students write to inquire whether or not the publication accepts student work, what their needs are and if payment can be expected, how much. Once the replies have been received, a class directory can be compiled for easy reference.

Collect sample copies of other magazines and examine them to find out the type of writing that they publish. (*Reader's Digest* is a good one to begin with.) This is important to do before deciding which magazine to submit work to.

Pretend that you have written one of the articles in one of the magazines that you have collected. Write the query letter that the real author could have written to that magazine six months ago in order to get his/her article published.

MAGAZINE LISTING

Alive*   Box 179, St. Louis, MO 63166
Canadian Children's Magazine   4150 Braken Ave., Victoria V8X 3N8 Canada
Chart Your Course*   PO Box 6448, Mobile, AL 36660-0448
Chickadee   59 Front Street E., Toronto, Ont. M5E 1B3, Canada
Child Life   1100 Waterway Boulevard, Indianapolis, IN 46206
Children's Digest   52 Vanderbilt Ave., New York, NY 10017
Children's House/Children's World   Box 111, Caldwell, NJ 07006
Children's Playmate   1100 Waterway Boulevard, Indianapolis, IN 46206
Creative Child and Adult Quarterly*   8080 Springvalley Dr., Cincinnati, OH 45236
Cricket Magazine*   Box 100, LaSalle, IL 61301
Discovery   999 College Ave., Winona Lake, IN 46590
Ebony Jr.   820 E. Michigan Ave., Chicago, IL 60605
The Friend   50 East North Temple, Salt Lake City, UT 84150
Highlights for Children   2300 W. Fifth Ave., Box 269, Columbus, OH 43216
Humpty Dumpty's Magazine   52 Vanderbilt Ave., New York, NY 10017
Instructor   757 Third Ave., New York, NY 10017
Jack and Jill   1100 Waterway Boulevard, Indianapolis, IN 46206
Merlin's Pen*   98 Main St., E. Greenwich, RI 02818
Owl   59 Front Street E., Toronto, Ont. M5E 1B3 Canada
Plays, The Drama Magazine for Young People   8 Arlington St., Boston, MA 02116
Prism*   900 E. Broward Boulevard, Ft. Lauderdale, FL 33301
Radar   8121 Hamilton Ave., Cincinnati, OH 45231
Scholastic Magazines Inc.*   50 W 44th Street, New York, NY 10036
Scholastic Scope* (Student Writing)   50 W. 44th Street, New York, NY 10036

Sprint   50 W. 44th Street, New York, NY 10036
Seventeen*   850 3rd Ave., New York, NY 10022
Story Friend   Scottsdale, PA 15683
Stone Soup, The Magazine by Children   PO Box 83, Santa Cruz, CA 95063
Tiger Beat*   7060 Hollywood Blvd, No. 800, Hollywood, CA 90028
Tigers and Lambs*   2041 E. Waverly, Tuscon AZ 85719
The Vine   201 Eighth Ave., South Nashville, TN 37202
Wee Wisdom   Unity Village, MO 64065
Wonder Time   6401 The Paseo, Kansas City, MO 64131
Young Crusader   1730 Chicago Ave., Evanston, IL 60201

TIPS ON SUBMITTING MANUSCRIPTS

Get the editor's name right.

Type your manuscript. Double space it. Put your name and address on each page, (upper left-hand corner).

Include a cover letter with the manuscript. Include a sample illustration but *never* the finished artwork until the publisher requests it. Tell the publisher who you are and why you have written the piece. Mention the intended audience and perhaps why you chose this publisher.

Make sure that you have a copy of all work submitted.

If you have written a storybook for children, let the publisher know that you have a dummy copy available upon request. Don't send it until it's requested.

Include a self-addressed stamped envelope.

Expect to wait several weeks to 2 months for a reply. It's very common.

When submitting work to several publishers, keep track of when you sent manuscripts to them.

Rejections do not mean that what you have written is not good. Be prepared to be rejected. Every published writer has been rejected at some time. Hang in there!

When submitting poetry, put each poem on a separate page.

Proofread carefully. If there are too many mistakes, retype it.

Some publishers prefer a query letter before you submit work. Include a brief outline of the main idea and your intended treatment of it. You may also wish to tell something about yourself. If the publisher says that he is interested in your work that only means that it will be *considered* for publication.

Type both the query letter and the cover letter. Keep them brief.

ADDITIONAL RESOURCES AND INFORMATION
(AVAILABLE AT MANY LIBRARIES)

Dorrance & Co.
Dept. ED-90
828 Lancaster Ave
Bryn Mawr, PA 19010
(Write for FREE booklet entitled *Author's Guide to Publication*   a subsidy book publisher)

Writer's Digest
205 West Center Street
Marion, OH 43305
(Write for FREE reprint of the article *Does It Pay To Pay To Have It Published*? Include SASE)

Vantage Press, Inc.
Dept. AA383
516 West 34th Street
New York, NY 10001
(Write for FREE copy of *To The Author In Search Of A Publisher*   a subsidy book publisher)

Available from: The Writer, Inc., 8 Arlington St., Boston, MA 02116

The Writer's Handbook("What's to write, How to write it, Where to sell it," lists over 2000 markets for manuscripts and includes an informative collection of articles by established writers)

Available from: Writers Digest Books, 933 Alliance Road, Cincinnati, OH 45242
The Creative Writer (excellent resource for writers established in creative writing and those beginning its practice)

Beginning Writer's Answer Book (answers to 500 frequently asked questions)

Writer's Market (annual) (lists over 4000 markets for manuscripts as well as detailed information on same)

A Complete Guide to Marketing (ideas for article development and selling potential)

Available from: National Council of Teachers of English, 1111 Kenyon Road, Urbana, IL 61801
Creative Writing in the Classroom (special resource section includes student writing contests, student-written anthologies, and magazines that publish student work)

Available from: Dustbooks, PO Box 1056, Paradise, CA 95969
International Directory of Little Magazines and Small Presses (annual) (a directory which lists and given information for submissions on over 2500 little magazines and small presses; comprehensive)

CHAPTER THIRTEEN

Content Area Writing

There are many activities throughout the book that can be used for writing in the content area. I have tried to suggest ideas along the way and I'm sure that if you give it some thought you can think of many more. I encourage all teachers to try to begin to use writing as a way to teach *thinking* and communication of ideas in their subject area. This does not have to mean long essays to correct or giving up *precious class time* either. Writing can be just one more way to motivate students to learn. As a teacher of math and science for the last seven years, I can honestly say that I have used all types of writing to teach these subjects and my students have never suffered or fallen behind because of the time spent. As a matter of fact, I feel that retention is greater and, when writing is combined with research, it has made the learning experience more enjoyable.

First you, the teacher, must decide what the learning objectives are to be. Perhaps you want students to know the facts and that is all; or maybe you would like them to analyze or synthesize factual information and draw some conclusions about what has been presented. Once decided, think of a range of choices that you have to offer to them (see Discourse Forms for Content Writing) in the way of writing activities that will allow them to demonstrate what they know. At first keep it short and simple, (i.e. bumper sticker, slogan, formula poem or telegram). Later you may wish to try some eye witness stories, letters, diaries or expository writing. No matter what the length of the writing done, requiring students to write helps them to organize, synthesize and therefore truly comprehend the subject matter. There is a difference between explaining something and explaining something *to* someone. Writing gives students an opportunity to communicate their knowledge to an audience. The audience may be real or imaginary or from the past, present or future. Who the audience is is not as important as the fact that there *is* an audience.

In content area writing the focus should be on the content. Writing assignments should provide students with the opportunity to be creative with the facts without changing them. My writing assignments in Science always require some research first, (i.e. Given the following items, keep a diary describing how you would survive for two weeks on the tundra, or make a travel brochure for one of the biomes studied. Make sure to include at least one vertebrate, one invertebrate, one flowering plant, etc. that a tourist wouldn't want to miss seeing there.)

Letters and news articles are great for content writing. Below is a sample of a letter written to a character in a story telling him something that you cannot tell him in person. This activity works well with any famous person in history, (i.e. scientists, mathematicians, etc.) This one was written by teacher, Dorothy Ramundo to Brutus from Artemidorus. See for yourself if the content of the reading doesn't come out in the letter.

Dear Brutus,

I feel that I must write to you because you've made a terrible mistake in judgement. You never should have joined the conspirators. Can't you see that Cassius and the rest of them are just using you? They needed a name, someone noble to make their plan seem right to the people. Oh, I know. People say you're gullible and naive. You're so honest yourself that you can't believe that anyone else could do wrong. You're planning this for the good of Rome. Don't kill Caesar! He's not so bad, Brutus. Read his will. He loves the people.

I could never tell you this to your face, yet I had to tell you: get out of this before it's too late...before the Ides of March. If you don't, you'll change the whole course of history.

Your worried friend,
Artemidorus

Guided fantasies are another way to approach content area writing. One idea is to write a guided fantasy that teaches a specific concept. This is called a guided cognitive imagery. There are many of these in *Mind Sight* and *200 Ways of Using Imagery in the Classroom* that might fit your needs; or you can follow the simple guidelines in this book for writing a guided fantasy. Students can image the fantasy and later write about their experiences, such as becoming a chloroplast during photosynthesis or building the Great Wall of China. A variation to this is to let the students write their own guided cognitive imageries. You may ask them to describe a scene from a story, an event in history or what it feels like to *be* a particular number or element. There is no way to do this without an understanding of the content. Here is a guided cognitive imagery written by a student, describing a scene from the novel, *Les Miserables*. Students were given two scenes to choose from after reading them in the book. They had also had the experience of guided fantasies and relaxation imageries before being asked to write one of their own.

Jean Valjean Rescues Marius
  by Donnel Brown, Grade 10

Relax...close your eyes...make yourself comfortable...see yourself entangled in the midst of war...feel the hate when you come upon a wounded man...you'd rather see him die...bend down...touch this warm yet cold, solemn body...feel the anguish...feel the guilt...feel the strain of being caught between right and wrong...left and right...good and bad...lift the body up onto your shoulders...(longer pause)...see yourself going down a damp, cold, underground passageway...notice that it is becoming dimmer...stand motionless in the dark...you can hardly see...you can't see...you are blind...let your eyes adjust to the light...remember that you are still in the passage...listen...shhhhh...hush...listen to the deep, absolute silence of night...feel your knees begin to shake as you struggle through the thick deep slime...it's like a pool of quicksand...feel the suction underneath as the weight of this hateful man pushes you even deeper...your legs feel like a ball and chain are wrapped around them...see a dim glimmer of light at the end of the tunnel...whisper a sigh of relief...notice a dark shadow hovering over the opening...wonder to yourself...who might it be?...is it a friend...or foe...

Here are some other suggestions for writing in the content area:
—Read over the activities in the sections on Science Fiction, Historical Fiction and Biographical Fiction.
—Instead of a report, try *Homage to* _____, honoring the subject of your tribute, no matter how common. It may be a person, object or place. Include the history of it, significance of it now and in the future, etc.
—Take a quote that is famous. Write about the circumstances that led to it becoming someone's famous last words. This makes a great Halloween bulletin board, the writing mounted on tombstone-shaped paper.
—Keep a class journal for observations and experiments. On the left, take notes on what happened. On the right, record personal reactions and questions and conclusions.

—Write letters to the chamber of commerce of a city that you are studying to ask for information about it.

—Write a letter to a museum asking for information on a particular exhibit that relates to your current unit of study.

—Write interview questions for someone in a career in which you are interested. Then conduct the interview over the phone at a time convenient for both of you.

—Write a week's menu for a particular group of people that you are studying.

—Write a letter of complaint to a company. Get the address from the product's package.

—Compile a list of products which are all marketed by the same company. Get this information by reading the labels.

—Compare the ingredients in products by reading labels. Make graphs that show percentages of sugar in various cereals, water in products, etc.

—Conduct a poll or survey. You choose the topic. Write up the results in an article. Include a graph.

—Have the class divide up into research teams. Give them all the same question. See which group can produce the most comprehensive treatment of the topic given. This includes models, diagrams, oral presentation, etc. *DON'T* teach anything about the topic. Make them start from scratch. By the time each team has made their presentation, most will have learned what you want them to know and they'll have done it on their own!

—Make an original game that teaches the main concepts found in one of the units of study. (This is great for end of the year review.) Questions should not all be trivial facts but also require application of fact, analysis and synthesis.

—Rather than a report, write a diary from the point of view of being the topic, (i.e. I am a dolphin, I am Henry VIII, I am World War II). Depending on what the topic is, determine the number of entries and time frame between them.

—Have students write about abstract concepts such as infinity.

—Have student write directions for conducting a particular experiment or an experiment that they would like to conduct to prove or disprove a concept or theory.

—Have students compare a chemical reaction to something that happens inside their minds in a particular situation.

—Have students list the items in a time capsule for a given people or time and then recreate the contents for others to guess the owners.

—Make a jump-rope rhyme that teaches a concept.

—Write a speech that will convince someone that a particular concept is easy to understand, (i.e. Logarithms are a Piece of Cake).

—Write rhyming couplets for factual information.

—Make a calendar of predictions using an almanac.

—Write an explanation why a superstition cannot be true.

—Rather than writing a report, compare what two sources say about the same topic.

—Write a review of a Science or History program seen on T.V.

—Write the script for your own T.V. documentary, the topic being the current unit of study.

—Use Word Synthesis or Picture/word Synthesis to write captions for pictures cut from magazines and newspapers. The words should be selected from a vocabulary list.

—Write a telegram containing the main idea of a reading assignment.

—Write acrostic or concrete poems about objects, elements, or artifacts.

—Write a contrast poem to demonstrate physical or chemical change in Science, the result of an operation in Mathematics or a new form of government in Social Studies.

—Write Haiku poems about plants or endangered species of animals.

—Write a ballad about a specific culture.

—Write an argument convincing a skeptic that one number is more important than another.
—Write the biography or autobiography of an object, number or substance from your unit of study.
—Write an advertisement for an object, number or substance from your unit of study.

SUGGESTED FORMULAS FOR CONTENT AREA WRITING

Title: Famous Person or Who Am I?

Line #1: Three adjectives that describe the person (physically)
Line #2: Person's claim to fame
Line #3: Three or four words that describe personality
Line #4: Detail about early life

* * * *

(Speak as a person seeing an event or as a famous person)

Line #1: I saw _____
Line #2: (where) _____
Line #3: (when) _____
Line #4: (what was happening) _____
Line #5: Two words that describe the action _____ and _____
Line #6: Making me feel _____

* * * *

Line #1: If I could be (object) _____
Line #2: I would _____ (describe appearance)
Line #3: Three action words that describe what you would do as the object _____,
_____, _____.
Line #4: People who saw me would _____
Line #5: Because _____

* * * *

Line #1: Concept (i.e. slavery, mitosis)
Line #2: Verb
Line #3: Adverb
Line #4: Reason why
Line #5: Adjective *or* Synonym *or* Antonym *or* Exclamation that refers back to the concept in Line #1.

* * * *

(To describe cause and effect.)

Line #1: If I were _____
Line #2: I would _____
Line #3: And (tell result) _____

DISCOURSE FORMS FOR CONTENT WRITING

ads
  for magazines
  for newspapers
  for yellow pages
advice columns
allegories
anecdotes
announcements
answers
anthems
appendices
applications
apologies
assumptions
autobiographies
awards

ballads
beauty tips
bedtime stories
beginnings
billboards
biographies
bloopers
blurbs
books
book jackets
book reviews
brochures
bulletins
bumper stickers

calendar quips
calorie charts
campaign speeches
cartoons
captions
case studies
  school problems
  local issues
  national concerns
  scientific issues
  historical problems

cereal boxes
certificates
character sketches
church bulletins
collages
commentaries
community bulletins
couplets
comparisons
comic strips
complaints
constitutions
contracts
conundrums
conversations
critiques
crossword puzzles
cumulative stories

data sheets
definitions
demonstrations
descriptions
dialogues
diaries
dictionaries
diets
directions
directories
documents
doubletalk
dramas
dream scripts

editorials
epilogues
epitaphs
encyclopedia entries
endings
essays
evaluations
exaggerations
exclamations
explanations

fables
fact books
fairy tales
fantasies
fashion articles
fashion show scripts
folklore
fortunes
futuristics
  careers
  employment
  education
  military
  technology

gags
game rules
graffiti
good news-bad news
greeting cards
grocery lists
gossip

headlines
historical stories
  you were there
horoscopes
how-to-do-it speeches

impromptu speeches
indexes
inquiries
insults
interviews
introductions
  to people
  to places
  to books
invitations

jingles
job applications
jokes
journals
jump rope rhymes

lab reports
labels
legends
letters

personal reactions
observations
public/persuasive
to imaginary people
from imaginary places
lies
lists
love notes
luscious words
lyrics

magazines
marquee notices
memories
metaphors
menus
memos
monologues
movie reviews
movie scripts
mysteries
myths
news analyses
newscasts
newspapers
   fillers
   letters
   articles
nonsense
notebooks
nursery rhymes

obituaries
observations
odes
opinions

palindromes
pamphlets
parables
parodies
party tips
persuasive letters
phrases
plays
poems
post cards
posters

prayers
problems
problem solutions
proformas
profound sayings
prologues
prophecy/prediction
proposals
propaganda sheets
protest signs
protest letters
product descriptions
proverbs
puppet shows
puns
puzzles

quips
quizzes
questionnaires
questions
quotations

radio plays
ransom notes
reactions
real estate notices
rebuttals
recipes
record covers
remedies
reports
requests
requiems
requisitions
resumes
reviews
revisions
rhymes
riddles

sale notices
sales pitches
satires
schedules
science fiction

school newspaper
secrets
self descriptions
sentences
sequels
serialized stories
sermons
signs
silly sayings
skywriting messages
slogans
soap operas
society news
songs/ballads
speeches
spoofs
spook stories
spoonerisms
sports accounts
sports analyses
superstitions

TV commercials
TV guides
TV programs
tall tales
technical reports
telegrams
telephone directories
textbooks
thank you notes
theater programs
thumbnail sketches
   of famous people
   of places
   of ideas/concepts
   of historical events
titles
tongue twisters
traffic rules
transcripts
travel folders
travel posters
tributes
trivia

used car descriptions

vignettes
vitas

want ads
wanted posters
warnings
wills
wise sayings
wishes
weather reports
weather forecasts
WORDS

yarns
yellow pages

—WHAT DO YOU SEE?

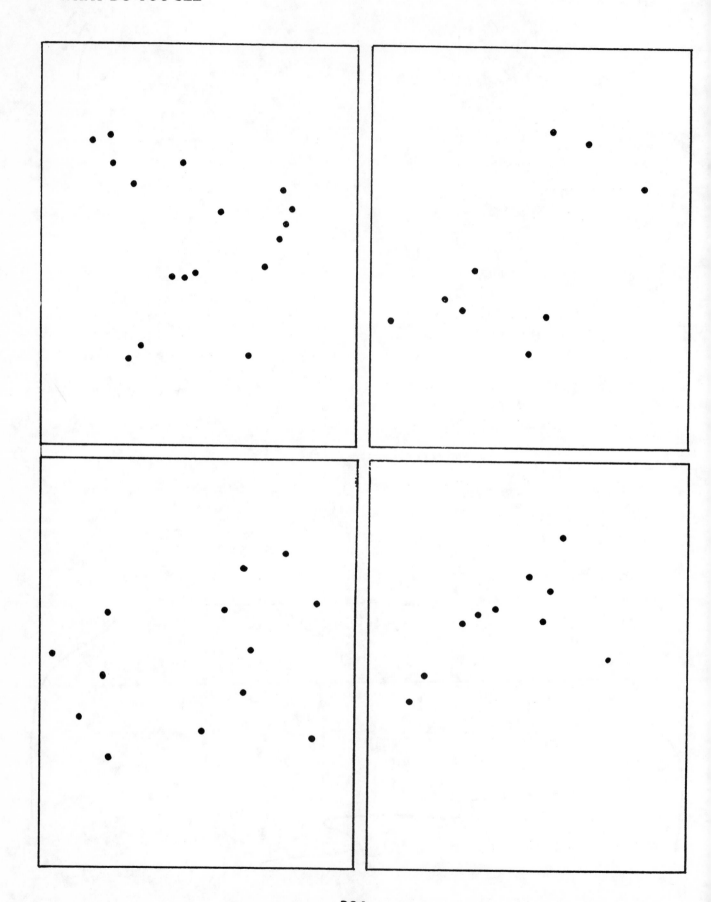

APPENDIX

APPENDIX

PICTURES FROM THE PAST

Below is a list of people, places or events that you may have experienced as a child. Read each one and then try to describe it as the child in you remembers it. If you have no memory to describe, go on to the next one. You may wish to reread your responses and add or revise them when you finish the list.

AN OLD LADY

EATING AN
ICE CREAM CONE

CLIMBING A TREE

A BIRTHDAY PARTY

A SONG YOU SANG

A TEACHER YOU
LOVED OR HATED

A PARK

A VACATION OR TRIP

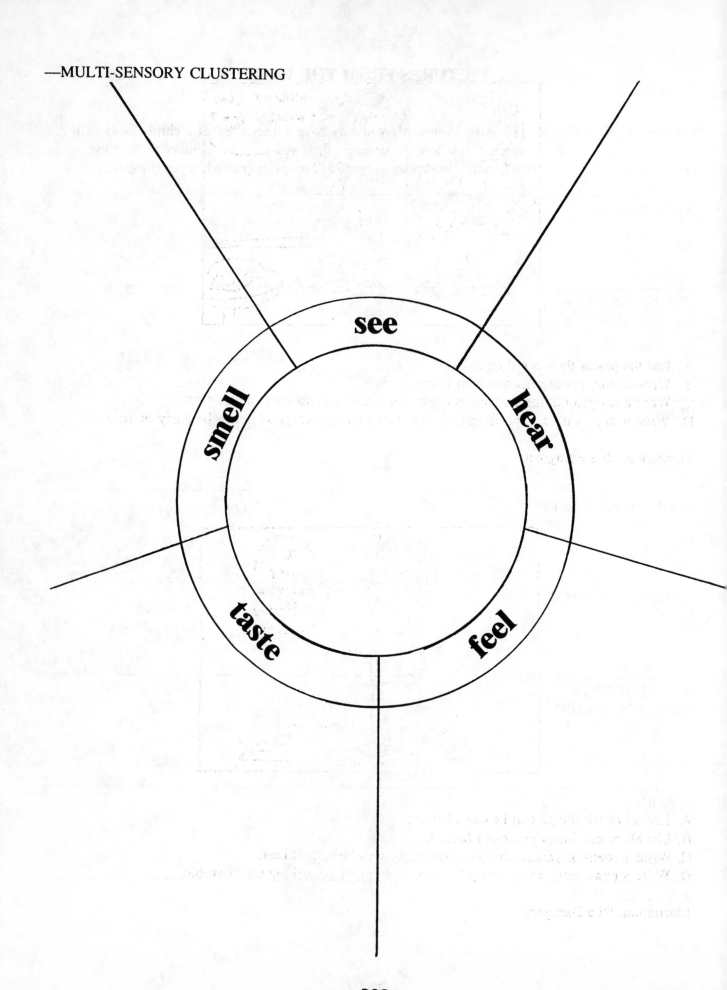

A. List the places they could be going.
B. Write a story about someone who is *never* ready.
C. Write a story about the day that no one was ready, so you went alone.
D. Write a story with a surprise ending that shows that it was *good* not to be ready on time.

Illustration, Rita Baragona

A. List all of the things that he can't believe.
B. List all of the things you can't believe.
C. Write a poem or paragraph about one of the unbelievable things.
D. Write a news story about an eye witness sighting of something unbelievable.

Illustration, Rita Baragona

A. Who is he speaking to and what's the idea?
B. Make a *long* list of your great ideas about making school better; making the world better; communicating with parents.
C. Write a story or poem, *The Great Idea*.
D. List the great ideas of a famous person. Then write about the greatest one.

Illustration, Rita Baragona

A. What has just happened? What will happen next? Draw and write.
B. Write a song for the cat, *Nobody Cares*. Sing it to a familiar tune.
C. Have you ever felt like the cat? Describe that time in a short story.
D. Write a want ad for the cat, describing his desirable qualities so someone *will* care about him.
Illustration, Rita Baragona

A. Make a list of things that always happen to you.
B. Write about one of those things but give it an unusual, silly, strange or surprising twist.
C. Make a list of things that always happen to this boy in school. Include both positive and negative things.
D. The paper is a response to his letter to Santa. What does it say?

Illustration, Rita Baragona

A. Draw and write about the reasons he is giving for *not*: doing his homework; paying attention; wanting to go home; wanting to go to the principal's office.
B. Write a story, *The Best Excuse*. Go into great detail describing the events and your feelings.

Illustration, Rita Baragona

A. Recreate the paper that is making him sigh.
B. Create a paper that would make you sigh.
C. Pretend the paper is a note or letter. Who is it from? What does it say? Why was it written? What will happen next?
D. Write a variety of dialogues that could follow this frame. Include these emotions: pride, disgust, confusion, disbelief, humor.

Illustration, Rita Baragona

A. Fill in the dialogue to show the following: The girl in the front is upset; conceited; being silly; looking at a blank paper. The girl in the back is asking a question; about to do something silly; being sarcastic; answering a question.
B. Draw what happened before and what will happen next.
C. Recreate the teacher's comments on the paper; and then fill in the girl's dialogue as response to seeing it.

Illustration, Rita Baragona

WRITING A TREATMENT
(PAGE 1)

TITLE   _____

NARRATIVE DESCRIPTION (Briefly describe the story line)   _____

_____

_____

_____

_____

CHARACTERS (List all characters and their main roles)
   CHARACTER   ROLE

_____

_____

_____

_____

_____

_____

_____

_____

SETTING (Describe each setting. Indicate whether or not it is an outside (O) or inside (I) location)

_____

_____

_____

_____

_____

_____

_____

_____

_____

LOCATION OF SHOOT (For each setting above, indicate where it will be shot. If the scene will be shot in the studio, list major props needed.)

_____

_____

_____

_____

TARGET AUDIENCE   _____

MOOD TO BE CREATED   _____

SPECIAL TECHNIQUES (List any tricky shots you may need to work out. Make a note of any scenes that may require special lighting or sound effects.)

_____

_____

_____

_____

_____

SOUND TRACT (List any special music/recordings/sound effects that will be needed.)

_____

_____

_____

_____

_____

TALENT (List the actors who will play the parts listed on page 1.)

_____

_____

_____

_____

_____

FRAME #

VISUAL

- -

AUDIO

- -

NARRATION

FRAME #

VISUAL

- -

AUDIO

- -

NARRATION

Visual

Describe what is happening in the scene. Include directions for the cameras (ECU, CU, ZOOM IN, ZOOM OUT, PAN, MS, LS, FADE OUT, FADE IN). For example: *LS of pond; PAN left to farmhouse*.

Audio

Describe music/sound effects. For example: *Birds singing*.

Narration

All speaking parts. Indicate who is speaking as in a play.

ONOMATOPOEIA WORD LIST

Below are some words that suggest the sound associated with them. Add more to the list as you think of them.

beat	gobble	sizzle	yap
blare	gong	slap	yelp
bump	grind	slip	yowl
buzz	grumble	slide	
	gush	slurp	zing
chime		sparkle	zip
chirp	hiss	spit	zoom
chop	howl	splash	
clack	hush	splatter	
clap		squeak	
click	jingle	stumble	
cluck			
coo	lap	thump	
creak		tingle	
crisp	moan	tinkle	
crunch	moo	tweet	
crush		twinkle	
	pop	twitch	
ding	purr	twitter	
dong			
drip	roar	whimper	
drizzle	rumble	whine	
drone		whisper	
drop	scratch	whistle	
	screech	whiz	
explode	shot	wobble	
	shriek		
fizzle	shrill		
flap	shush		

CHARACTER DEVELOPMENT

Name _____

Age _____ Education _____

Marital Status _____ Children _____

Family Background _____
_____

Present Residence _____
_____

Occupation _____

Special Skills _____
_____
_____

Hobbies _____
_____

Physical Characteristics:
Hair _____
Eyes _____
Height _____
Clothing _____
_____

DISTINGUISHING FEATURES _____

VOICE (accents/tone/etc.) _____
_____

Manner Of Movement _____
_____

Personality Traits:
Positive (things you admire about the character) _____
_____

Negative (things that you do not admire or even dislike) _____
_____

CAUSE AND EFFECT

EVENTS	ACTIONS		REACTIONS
SETTING & MAIN CHARACTER	OF MAIN CHARACTER	OF OTHER CHARACTERS	OF CHARACTERS IMMEDIATE...LONG TERM

CHARACTER DESCRIPTORS

able
accepting
adaptable
aggressive
ambitious
annoying
anxious
authoritative
bitter
boring
bold
brave
bubbly
calm
carefree
careless
caring
certain
cheerful
clever
cold
complex
confident
conforming
courageous
cranky
creative
critical
demanding
dependable
dependent
determined
dignified
diplomatic
disciplined
efficient
egotistical
fair
fearful
foolish
frank
free

friendly
full of life
funny
gentle
giving
greedy
guilty
gullible
happy
hard
helpful
helpless
honorable
hostile
humorous
idealistic
imaginative
immature
impressionable
inconsiderate
independent
insensitive
insincere
intelligent
irresponsible
irritable
jealous
juvenile
kind
knowledgeable
lazy
liberal
lively
logical
loving
materialistic
maternal
mature
merry
modest
moody
naive

negative
nervous
noisy
normal
objective
observant
organized
original
overconfident
overconforming
overemotional
overprotecting
overworked
overly sensitive
passive
patient
perceptive
perfectionist
persuasive
petty
playful
pleasant
powerful
practical
precise
pretending
protective
proud
questioning
quiet
rational
rationalizing
realistic
reasonable
reassuring
rebellious
rejecting
relaxed
reliable
religious
resentful
respectful

responsible
responsive
rigid
sarcastic
satisfied
scientific
searching
self-aware
self-conscious
selfish
sensible
sensitive
sentimental
serious
shy
silly
simple
skillful
sly
sociable
spontaneous
stable
strong
strong-willed
stubborn
sympathetic
tender
tense
thoughtful
tough
trusting
trustworthy

unaware
uncertain
unconcerned
understanding
unpredictable
unreasonable
useful
vain
vulnerable

warm
wise
wishful
withdrawn
witty
worried
youthful

PLOT IDEAS

These capsulized summaries came directly from newspaper articles. They may be used for plays, realistic fiction, fantasy stories, or news articles. Ideas may be cut apart or used as is.

- - - -

An unknown person cut a hole in the back of the building used by attorney D. Lockwood to gain entry to the storage space there. Files were removed. File drawers were thrown on the floor.

- - - -

A Turkish hijacker surrendered to anti-terrorist police who rushed him after he released 114 people. The hijacker was armed with a knife and bottle filled with an unidentified substance. No one was hurt.

- - - -

Six Air Force planes searched the mountains and canyons for an unarmed B-52 bomber that disappeared during a practice run. There were seven crew members.

- - - -

Billi H., mother of a critically ill boy, Brandon, went before a Congressional subcommittee to plead for aid to cover liver transplant costs. The search for a donor weighting less than 20 pounds was successful and the 12 hour operation was performed.

- - - -

Christopher K., father of twin boys and a younger sister dashed through eight foot flames to save his children. He sustained second and third degree burns, but was not aware of the fire or pain until afterward.

- - -

Charles B. was working under his truck in the garage when the jack slipped, pinning him beneath. His four-year-old son, Brandon, replaced the handle and pumped until the truck was off of his father. He next grabbed his father's foot and pulled until the rolling platform moved from under the truck.

- - - -

One year after he was pronounced *technically dead*, Jimmy walked away from Chicago's Children's Memorial Hospital. The 5 ½ year old was rescued from icy Lake Michigan after being submerged for about 20 minutes. He completely recovered from the accident.

- - - -

An explosion flattened part of a 3-story hotel-restaurant at a mountain ski resort, trapping a 12 year old girl. Her hand was pinned beneath a concrete block; she was unconscious. Amputation could be necessary to save her life.

- - - -

Villa, a 1-year-old Newfoundland, dug out a young girl trapped in a snowbank and dragged the girl 40 feet to her Villas, NJ home.

- - - -

A New York mixed breed puppy kept a 2-year-old girl warm during the night until searchers found her.

- - - -

A California Labrador retriever-Irish setter mix saved a man from drowning.

- - - -

A Wisconsin collie protected a man from an attacking bear.

- - - -

A Michigan German shepherd found and brought help for a woman seriously injured when she fell off a horse.

- - - -

Lady, a German shepherd, saved her master, Burnie W. from a charging 600 pound hog. The sow charged when he was chasing her six piglets.

- - - -

A family's pet pig swam to save a drowning 6-year-old girl who was pulled to safety by holding its collar.

- - - -

CHART FOR COLORS AND SHAPES

Dark   Matter, germ, before existence, chaos

Light   Spirit, morality, All, creative force, the direction East, spiritual thought

Red   Sunrise, birth, blood, fire, emotion, wounds, death, passion, sentiment, mother, Mars, the note *C*, anger, excitement, heat, physical stimulation

Orange   Fire, pride, ambition, egoism, Venus, the note *D*

Yellow   Sun, light, intuition, illumination, air, intellect, royalty, Mercury, the note *E*, luminosity

Green   Earth, fertility, sensation, vegetation, death, water, nature, sympathy, adaptability, growth, Jupiter and Venus, the note *G*

Blue   Clear sky, thinking, the day, the sea, height, depth, heaven, religious feeling, devotion, innocence, truth, psychic ability, spirituality, Jupiter, the note *F*, physical soothing and cooling

Violet   Water, nostalgia, memory, advanced spirituality, Neptune, the note *B*

Circle   Heaven, intellect, thought, sun, the number two, unity, perfection, eternity, oneness, the masculine-active principle, celestial realm, hearing, sound

Triangle   Communication, between heaven and earth, fire, the number three, trinity, aspiration, movement upward, return to origins, gas, sight, light

Square   Pluralism, earth, feminine-receptive principle, firmness, stability, construction, material, solidity, the number four

Rectangle   Most rational, most secure

Spiral   Evolution of the universe, orbit, growth, deepening, cosmic motion, relationship between unity and multiplicity, macrocosm, breath, spirit, water

Cross   Tree of life, axis of the world, ladder, struggle, martyrdom, orientation in space

CHART OF COMMON SYMBOLS

Air   Activity, male primary element, creativity, breath, light, freedom, liberty, movement

Ascent   Height, transcendence, inward journey, increasing intensity

Center   Thought, unity, timelessness, spacelessness, paradise, creator, infinity, neutralizing opposites

Descent   Unconscious, potentialities of being, animal nature

Duality   Opposites, complements, positive-negative, male-female, life-death

Earth   Passive, feminine, receptive, solid

Eye   Understanding, intelligence, sacred fire, creative

Fire   Ability to transform, love, life, health, control, spiritual energy, regeneration, sun, God, passion

Image   Highest form of knowing, thought as a form

Lake   Mystery, depth, unconscious

Moon   Master of women, vegetation

Mountain   Height, mass, loftiness, center of the world, ambition, goals

Sun   Hero, son of heaven, knowledge, the Divine eye, fire, life force, creative-guiding force, brightness, splendor, active awakening, healing, resurrection, ultimate wholeness

Unity   Spirit, oneness, wholeness, transcendence, the source, harmony, revelation, active principle, a point, a dot, supreme power, completeness in itself, light, the divinity

Water   Passive, feminine

CHART OF GREEK AND ROMAN MYTHOLOGY

Greek	Roman	Position
Aphrodite	Venus	Goddess of love
Apollo	Apollo	God of light, medicine, and poetry
Ares	Mars	God of war
Artemis	Diana	Goddess of hunting and childbirth
Asclepius	Aesculaplus	God of healing
Athena	Minerva	Goddess of crafts, war, and wisdom
Cronus	Saturn	In Greek mythology, ruler of the Titans and father of Zeus; in Roman mythology, also the god of agriculture
Demeter	Ceres	Goddess of growing things
Dionysus	Bacchus	God of wine, fertility, and wild behavior
Eros	Cupid	God of love
Gaea	Terra	Symbol of the earth and mother and wife of Uranus
Hephaestus	Vulcan	Blacksmith for the gods and god of fire and metalworking
Hera	Juno	Protector of marriage and women. In Greek mythology, sister and wife of Zeus; in Roman mythology, wife of Jupiter
Hermes	Mercury	Messenger for the gods; god of commerce and science, and protector of travelers, thieves and vagabonds
Hestia	Vesta	Goddess of the hearth
Hypnos	Somnus	God of sleep
Pluto, or Hades	Pluto	God of the underworld
Poseidon	Neptune	God of the sea. In Greek mythology, also god of earthquakes and horses
Rhea	Ops	Wife and sister of Cronus
Uranus	Uranus	Son and husband of Gaea and father of the Titans
Zeus	Jupiter	Ruler of the gods

CONNECTORS

CONNECTORS are transitional words and phrases that are used to connect or tie the ideas of a composition together. Add any new ones to the list that you think of.

all in all	hereafter	really
also	however	so
but		should
because	in addition to	since
connsequently	indeed	sometimes
consider this	in conclusion	surely
conversely	most assuredly	
	mostly	then
definitely		therefore
	needless to say	thus
eventually	nevertheless	truthfully
everything considered	next	
	not only	ultimately
finally	notwithstanding	
first		when
for	occasionally	whereas
for instance	of course	
fortunately		while
furthermore	perhaps	without a doubt
generally	possibly	with that in mind
generally speaking	probably	
	prior to	yet
	quite	

Writing Skills Checklist

Name _____ Grade _____

Teacher _____

Check after a student has demonstrated mastery of each skill. Check each time it is demonstrated until three checks are recorded.

1. Uses varied language
2. Uses vivid language
3. Uses alliteration
4. Uses similes
5. Uses metaphors
6. Correct word usage
7. Correct verb tense
8. Correct subject/verb agreement
9. Third person
10. First person
11. Complete sentences
12. Varied sentences
13. Parallel Form
14. Comes full circle
15. Unifying thread
16. Effective rhythmic flow
17. Correct punctuation
18. Correct spelling
19. Point of View
20. Clarity of thought
21. Effective transitions
22.
23.
24.
25.

Creative Writing Inventory

Name _____ Grade _____ Date _____

This assessment is for the purpose of determining how you get your ideas for writing, what you find easy and difficult about writing and how you think you can improve your writing ability. Answer all questions...Even if you have to say *I don't know* .

1. Do you have a best time for writing?   When?

2. Do you have a best place for writing?   Where?

3. Are there any special conditions that enhance your ability to write?

4. How do you get your ideas for writing? (playing with words, reading, thinking of *nothing at all, fantasizing, daydreaming, when I feel good or bad, when it's assigned, seeing a movie, etc.*)

5. What do you find most difficult about writing?

6. If you could find an easier way to do something related to writing, what would it be? (use unusual words, evoke feelings, be more original or clever, create vividness, etc.)

7. What would you call your best asset in writing? (advanced vocabulary, creative ideas, etc.)

8. What do you feel you'd like to develop in order to improve your writing ability?

9. What do you prefer to write? (poetry, short stories, dramatic scripts, etc.)

AFTER-IMAGES

HOW TO PREPARE THE TRANSPARENCIES

(1) Using the next page as your pattern, trace the center circle onto a clear acetate sheet.

(2) Color in the circle with RED marking pen or glue a circle of red cellophane to the acetate sheet. The darker the red, the better. You may have to color 2 layers of color.

(3) Follow the same procedure for BLUE, YELLOW and BLACK. Or for the BLACK, just glue a solid paper circle to the acetate. It will project as a black shadow.

(4) For the WHITE circle, simply cut a circle from a solid sheet of paper. When projected, it will look like a white circle on a black background.

Cut out circle: Use paper that surrounds the circle:

AFTER-IMAGES

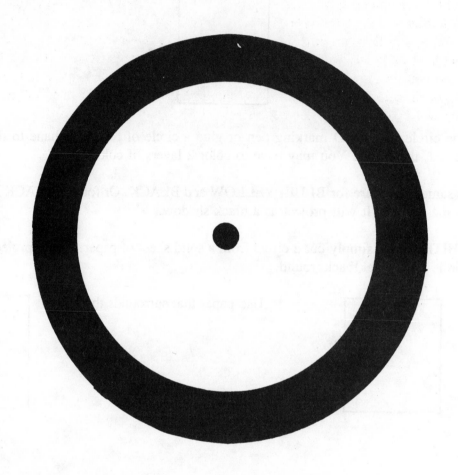

TRANSPARENCY

WORD CARDS

WORD CARDS are simply words written on cards. You can use 3x5 cards, but I prefer construction paper so that I can color code them in case I need to separate them for a particular activity. Because the words are on cards, you can divide the class up easily and assign words easily. I continue to add new words all of the time and students even suggest adding some to the pile. The words on the Character Descriptors Worksheet and the Onomatopoeia Word List will give you an excellent start. I also include colors, shapes and a long list of nouns. You may wish to add certain vocabulary words that need to be reinforced throughout the year. An easy way to get your word cards made is to ask the class to help you the first time you do an activity requiring word cards. It will take only a couple of minutes and will make students become familiar with the spelling of vocabulary words also. Try to include all parts of speech on the word cards. Try to use evocative words.

-NOTES-

PICTURE FILE

A PICTURE FILE is a collection of pictures of all shapes, sizes and subjects that I keep on hand at all times to use with writing. I have listed a variety of sources below that are wonderful for locating pictures. It doesn't matter what size the pictures are, since most of the time individual students will be using them. To make them look nicer, I glue them to colored construction paper and laminate. This also prolongs their life. Once you have collected a considerable amount, I suggest that you divide them into Settings and Characters. For settings, try to include: indoor and outdoor settings, unusual environments, famous sites, foreign sites, a variety of times of day and year as well as time periods. For your file folder on characters: people alone and with other people, animals, people of all ages and walks of life, objects, plants, and famous people. Sometimes libraries and museums will loan pictures out, also. Here are some places that I have gotten my pictures:

discarded library books
discarded magazines and newspapers
old calendars
junk mail ads for encyclopedias and text books
old text books
baseball cards
posters
greeting cards
postcards
catalogs
old photos
comic books and Sunday comics
old workbooks
coloring books
all of the above from friends and neighbors

PICTURE FILE

OUT-OF-FOCUS PICTURES

Out-of-focus pictures are pictures that really don't show anything. They leave much up to the mind to use what is given, usually color or shape, and create an image with it. They are more a motivational starting point than anything else. From the list below, you can see that size does not matter. Very small ones can be used by individual students, while slides can be projected for the entire class. I can guarantee that this part of your picture file can be created without any expense and very little time.

SUGGESTED SOURCES FOR FINDING AND CREATING OUT-OF-FOCUS PICTURES

1. Photographs and slides that did not print correctly
2. Dropping a few sprinkles of bleach onto a photograph or slide
3. Rubbing nail polish remover over a magazine's color ad or picture
4. Cutting a portion of a magazine photo, a calendar picture or newspaper photo that includes only part of the out-of-focus background
5. Wetting water color paper and dropping a few blobs of paint onto it to let it mix
6. Cutting a portion of a picture so that it is difficult to tell what the larger picture was (for example, from a nature magazine you can get a closeup of the bark of a tree or the scales of a fish)
7. Cutting narrow strips from a picture and pasting them together in a different way.
8. Cutting part of an object from a picture so that there is only one color showing (for example, cut a leaf or flower petal in the shape of a square, circle, triangle, etc. so as not to give it away)
9. Having your students create their own versions of OUT-OF-FOCUS pictures
10. Using collage, (collected objects) or montage, (mounted pictures) to generate a central theme— DON'T MAKE IT OBVIOUS! As a matter of fact, try to use unrelated and partial pictures and objects.

GLOSSARY OF RELATED TERMS

after-image: image seen after looking at a bright object against a dark background; cannot be scanned because the image shifts when the eyes move.

astral-travel: happens when a person has ordinary sense perceptions of actual things and persons from a point of view located outside the position occupied by his physical body; he may feel that during this time he has another body and is totally unaware of sensations to his physical body; out-of-body experience.

autohypnosis: the process by which a person can give himself the suggestions used to induce hypnosis; any exercise which involves the reader's repeating to himself verbal suggestions are techniques similar to autohypnosis.

automatic writing: after being hypnotized and given a pencil and paper, the inner mind is told to take over muscular control of the hands and write; used primarily in therapy in order to gain clues to traumatic memories.

automatic imaging: procedure that involves the following steps:
(1) choose a simple image (2) relax and shut eyes (3) let image go any way it wants to for one minute (4) open eyes (5) write about the image excursion, beginning with the one chosen.

autosuggestion: mentally saying to yourself that each part of the body is becoming relaxed, one by one (i.e. *my feet are relaxed...my ankles feel relaxed*, etc.) while breathing deeply and slowly in order to become more relaxed.

auto symbolizing: natural means by which the brain uses symbols for solving complex problems; during a hynagogic state, visual symbols are substituted for the components of an abstract problem or verbal data; three stages are: (1) become receptive and relaxed (2) introduce a problem (3) look for answers in the form of visualizations.

centering: process of clearing the mind of distractions that hinder the ability to image clearly; often begins with a slow deep breath and concentration on a *dot* or *star* in the center of the forehead.

clairvoyance: knowledge of an object or event without inference or known sensory means: ESP of objects and events.

complex image: image which required additional creative energy for its production; contains added details and elaborative features (i.e. frenzied, half-crazed husky hurling himself wildly at his attacker).

concentration: one-pointedness of mind; a mental state during conscious visualization where alertness, clarity of thought, identification with the object and a feeling of participation in the visualization are present; the person becomes less involved with himself as being separate from the world around him.

confluent imagery: a guided imagery which merges the components of at least two of the following: centering, cognitive mastery, awareness of inner life (affective) and transpersonal growth (transpersonal).

236

consciousness: state of being able to see and learn from the imagery vignettes passing through the mind.

cybernetics: a science which deals with with relationship between positive and negative messages in reaching a particular goal; based upon messages sent to the brain by the sense organs, the brain, in turn sends, nerve impulses to the muscles in order to attain the goal being pictured (i.e. picking up a pencil)

daydreams: combination of memory and imagination images usually experienced as a series of images, more or less in chronological order.

destructuring: process (used in problem solving) of pulling apart the elements of an image in order to reorganize them (see restructuring).

dream image: images that occur during sleep (between 3 and 5 per night) over which people have little or no control

eidectic image: a vision, a new thought or a feeling of unusual vividness which can be scanned by a person as he would scan a real event in the environment, most frequently experienced by school-age children.

extrasensory perception (ESP): response or awareness of an event not based on known sensory perception or logical, rational thought.

guided affective imagery: imagery used to develop personal skills, such as introspection, self-reflection, self-understanding, bonding, unity, trust, empathy, conflict resolution, self-concept, etc.

guided cognitive imagery: imagery used for the purpose of teaching basic subjects (science, math, etc.) as well as technical skills (carpentry, cooking, etc,).

guided imagery: process whereby individuals are led through spoken suggestions, to create in their minds a situation that corresponds to the theme given; insights and meanings may be generated from the images experienced.

guided transpersonal imagery: imagery used to explore expanded aspects of human intelligence and consciousness, including the intuitive, mystical, spiritual and cosmic realms of knowing.

hallucination: an extremely vivid image experienced by a person believing that it is occurring in the outer world (a similar visualization experienced as an internal picture would be an imagination image); conditions associated with causing hallucinations are fever, drugs, deprivation of food, etc.

hypnagogic imagery: train of images that occur in the twilight state just before falling asleep; brought about by the natural rhythm of waking and sleeping (see hypnopompic imagery).

hypnopompic imagery: images that occur in the twilight state before becoming fully awake; tend to be vivid, detailed and beyond the reach of conscious control (see hypnagogic images)

imagination image: image with no fixed reference point (does not necessarily relate to a specific event or situation); usually spontaneous and unstructured, integrating the past, present and future.

imaging: mental processing of information in non-verbal form; can occur freely or be made to occur by planned experiences.

mandala: complex design made of concentric circles, other geometric shapes and/or symbols and images of divinities; often used as concentration devices to aid visualization or meditation to thus experience the forces behind the forms.

mastery rehearsal: visualizing an upcoming event or physical activity in the absence of any gross muscular movement (i.e. practicing visualization of shooting free-throws in basketball); importance is on control of the image and the ability to *feel* as well as to *see* the activity being visualized.

meditation: process of undistracted focusing on inner images and feelings often resulting in new realizations about life.

memory image: previously experienced events or situations that may be spontaneously evoked by sensory stimuli (picture, taste, smell, verbal utterance, etc.) or summoned when trying to recall facts; most common type of visualization.

mental telepathy: transmission and/or reception of thoughts and mental states from one person to another, without inference or known sensory means; ESP of mental states.

out-of-body experience: (see astral travel)

precognition: ability to predict future events.

programmed visualization: a person holds a particular image in his mind and concentrates on it (see receptive visualization).

psychokinesis (PK): direct mental influence on material objects.

receptive visualization: a person spontaneously receives images (see programmed visualization).

recurrent image: an image that may reoccur after a scene has been experienced for a prolonged period of time (i.e. a driver staring at the highway): may occur either immediately after or several hours later; person has little control over this type of image.

reflective imaging: a train of images occurring either as hypnagogic or hypnopompic imagery which may be loosely or closely strung together in a linear series or organized in patterns related to the whole; requires (1) background to the content and (2) relaxation in order to be creative and productive; best suited to story writing, poetic composition, artistic expression, etc. (Examples in literature include: *Kubla Khan*, Coleridge; *Noddy Stories*, Enid Blyton; *Othello*, Shakespeare.)

restructuring: process (used in problem solving) of reorganizing the elements of an image to produce something new or combining other elements with it to produce something more original (see destructuring).

simple image: image which shows developmental features; need further imaging to become a complex image (i.e. *excited dog defending himself* as compared to *frenzied, half-crazed husky hurling himself wildly at his attacker*).

symbol: mechanism by which the brain makes meaning out of discrete pieces of information; that which can resolve paradoxes and create order from disorder, providing flashes of insight and expressing universal concepts which go beyond simple verbal explanations.

synaesthesia: (also synesthesia) the crossing of sensory experiences; sensory impressions registered in one modality are felt in all sensory modalities simultaneously, thus sounds have shape, color, taste, etc. (i.e. *hearing the approach of darkness*).

synthesis: combining images in a way that is unique, often taking place without our full awareness of it.

vision: (see hallucination)

yantra: simple mandala composed of triangles and other geometric shapes, having specific colors and mathematical proportions.

BIBLIOGRAPHY OF SUGGESTED READINGS

Ahsen, A. "Eidetics: An Overview". *Journal of Mental Imagery*, 1977, Vol.1, 5-37.

Ahsen, A. "Imagery Approach In The Treatment of Learning Disability." *Journal of Mental Imagery*, 1981, Vol. 5, 157-196.

Ahsen, A. *Psycheye:* Self-Analytic Consciousness. New York: Brandon House, 1977.

Allen, E. and Colbrunn, E. *The Student Writer's Guide,* Revised Edition. Deland, Florida: Everett/Edwards, Inc., 1980.

Andersen, U.S. *The Magic In Your Mind*. Wilshire Book Co., 1961.

Arya, P. *Mantra & Meditation*. Honesdale, PA.: Himalayan International Institute of Yoga, Science, and Philosophy, 1981.

Bagley, M. and Hess, K. *200 Ways of Using Imagery In The Classroom*. New York: Trillium Press, 1984.

Bandler, R. and Grindler, J. *Frogs Into Princes:* Neurolinguistic Programming. Moab, Utah: Real People Press, 1979.

Boswell, N. *Inner Peace, Inner Power*. New York: Ballantine Books, 1985.

Bry, Adelaide. *Visualization: Directing the Movies of Your Mind*. New York: Harper & Row, 1978.

Buzan, T. *Use Both Sides of Your Brain*. New York: Dutton, 1976.

Capacchione, L. *The Creative Journal*. Athens, Ohio: Swallow Press, 1979.

Cohen, K. *Imagine That*. Santa Barbara, CA.: Santa Barbara Books, 1983.

Cotter, P., Johansen, C., and Parr, J. *Dream Scenes*. Santa Barbara, CA.: The Learning Works, Inc., 1983.

Dayton, B. *The Swami and Sam,* a Yoga Book. Glenview, Ill.: Himalayan International Institute of Yoga, Science, and Philosophy, 1976.

DeMille, R. *Put Your Mother On The Ceiling*. New York: Penguin Books, 1973.

Edwards, B. *Drawing On The Right Side Of The Brain*. Los Angeles, CA.: J.P. Tarcher, Inc., 1979.

Ferguson, A. *The Aquarian Conspiracy*. Los Angeles, CA.: Tarcher, 1980.

Funderburk, J. *Science Studies Yoga*, A Review of Physiological Data. Honesdale, Pa.: Himalayan International Institute of Yoga, Science, and Philosophy, 1977.

Galyean, B. "Guided Imagery In Education." *Journal of Humanistic Psychology,* 1981, Vol. 21, 57-68.

Galyean, B. *Integrative Learning*. (90 minute tape), Santa Barbara, CA.: Center For Integrative Learning, 1980.

Galyean, B. *Mind Sight*. Santa Barbara, Ca.: Center For Integrative Learning, 1983.

Gawain, S. *Creative Visualization*. New York: Bantam New Age Books, 1982.

Gendlin, E. *Focusing*. New York: Bantam New Age Books, 1981.

Hills, C., and Rozman D. *Exploring Inner Space*. Boulder Creek, CA.: University of The Trees Press, 1978.

Henricks, G. and Wills, R. *The Centering Book*. Englewood Cliffs, NJ: Prentice-Hall, 1975.

Herzog, S. *Joy In The Classroom*. Boulder Creek, CA.: University Of The Trees Press, 1982.

Houston, J. *The Possible Human*. Los Angeles, CA.: J.P. Tarcher, Inc., 1982.

Individualized Language Arts (Jeanette Alder, Project Director). Wilson School, Hauxhurst Ave., Weehawken, NJ, 1973.

Khatena, J. Creative Imagination Imagery Actionbook. *Starkville, MS: Allen Associates, Inc., 1981.*

Khatena, J. "Creative Imagination Imagery and Analogy." Gifted Child Quarterly, 1975, Vol. 19, 2, 149-160.

Khatena, J. *Teaching Gifted Children To Use Creative Imagination Imagery*. Starkville, MS: Allen Associates, 1979.

LeShan, L. *How To Meditate*. New York: Bantam, 1975.

Maltz, Maxwell. *Psycho-Cubernetics*. North Hollywood, CA.: Wilshire Book Co., 1960.

Massy, R. *Hill's Theory Of Consciousness*. Boulder Creek, CA.: University Of The Trees Press, 1976.

Nin, A. *The Diary Of Anais Nin*, V.5. New York: Harcourt Brace, 1964.

Nuernberger, P. *Freedom From Stress*. Honesdale, PA.: Himalayan Institute, 1981.

Oaklander, V. *Windows To Our Children*. Moab, Utah: Real People Press, 1978.

Ostrander, S. and Schroeder, L. *Superlearning*. New York: Dell Publishing Co., 1979.

Paivio, A. *Imagery and Verbal Processes*. New York: Holt, Rinehart, & Winston, 1971.

Peale, N. *Positive Imaging*. New York: Ballantine Books, Random House, Inc., 1982.

Rama, S. *Exercise Without Movement,* Manual One. Honesdale, PA.:
The Himalayan International Institute of Yoga, *Science and Philosophy,* 1984.

Rama, S., Ballentine, R., and Hymes, A. *Science Of Breath.* Honesdale, Pa.: Himalayan International Institute of Yoga, Science, and Philosophy, 1979.

Rico, G. *Writing The Natural Way.* Los Angeles, CA.: J.P. Tarcher, Inc., 1983.

Rozman, D. *Meditating With Children.* Boulder Creek, CA.: University Of The Trees Press, 1975.

Russell, P. *The Brain Book.* New York: Hawthorne Books, 1979.

Samuels, M. and Samuels, N. *Seeing With The Mind's Eye.* New York: Random House, Inc., 1975.

Schultz, J. *Writing From Start To Finish.* Upper Montclair, NJ: Boynton Book Publishers, Inc. 1982.

Shorr, J. *Go See The Movie In Your Head.* New York: Popular Library, 1977.

Silverstein, Shel. *Where The Sidewalk Ends.* New York: Harper & Row, 1974.

Sommer, R. *The Mind's Eye.* New York: Dell Publishing Co., Inc., 1978.

Sperry, R. "Hemisphere Disconnection and Unity In Conscious Awareness." *American Psychologist,* 23 (2), 1968.

Torrance, E., Khatena, J., and Cunnington, B. *Thinking Creatively With Sounds And Words.* Bensenville, IL.: Scholastic Testing Service. 1973.

MUSIC AND/OR TAPE LISTINGS

COMPANY/ADDRESS

Center for Integrative Learning
207 West Mason
Santa Barbara, CA 93101

Effective Learning Systems, Inc.
5221 Edina Ind. Blvd.
Edina, MN 55435

Institute of Human Development
P.O. Box 1616
Ojai, CA 93023

New Age Music
Valley Of The Sun
Box 38
Malibu, CA 90265

Superlearning, Inc.
450 Seventh Avenue, Suite 500
New York, NY 10123

SUGGESTED TITLES

Galyean, Mindsight I: *Getting Started* (with imagery)
Galyean, Mindsight II: *Guided Cognitive Imageries*
(subject areas)
Galyean, Mindsight III: *Guided Affective Imageries*
Galyean, Mindsight IV: *Guided Transpersonal Imageries*
Galyean, *Integrative Learning:* Brain Research-Lecture

Comfort Zone: Keyboards and Strings
Kelly, *Ancient Echoes:* Harp and Keyboard
- evokes images of ancient Greece, Egypt, and China

The Pachelbel Canon: Plus other Baroque selections
Bergman, *Music For An Inner Journey:* Soft keyboard,
flute, and birds
Halpern, *Dawn:* Flutes and piano

Dreamscapes: Environmental sounds with strings and
synthesizer
Music For Imaging: Includes Beethoven, Debussy, and
Strauss
Largos and Adagios: Includes Vivaldi, Bach, and Molter

Bearns & Dexter, *Golden Voyage:* Nature sounds and
orchestral tones
Ostrander, *Superlearning Guided Imagery For Children:*
(pre K-grade 3) guided fantasy
Superlearning Music: Baroque style with
60 beat tempo for relaxation and factual learning

Syntonic Research
175 Fifth Avenue
New York, NY 10010

Environments: "Ocean/Lake"; "Wind In Trees/Ultimate Heart Beat"; "Sailboat"

The Soundworks, Inc.
911 N. Fillmore St.
Arlington, VA 22201

Rico, *Unleashing The Inner Writer:* Using Creative Ability - Lecture
Buzan, *Brain and Beyond:* Brain research - Lecture
Chinmoy, *Flute-Music For Meditation:* Flute

University of the Trees Press
P.O. Box 644
Boulder Creek, CA 95006

Rozman, *Meditating With Children:* Taped meditations (guided imageries)

INFORMATION AND ORGANIZATIONS

Brain/Mind Bulletin
Interface Press
P.O. Box 4211
Los Angeles, CA 90042

Center For Integrative Learning
207 West Mason
Santa Barbara, CA 93101

Gray Matter, Inc.
The PCS Group
New York, NY 10048

I.M.A.G.E. (Institute For Maximizing Affective Growth In Education)
P.O. Box 612
Portland, PA 18351

Journal Of Mental Imagery/International Imagery Assn.
P.O. Box 1046
Bronx, NY 10471

Pro Helios, Inc.
397 N. Broadway Suite 1-0
Yonkers, NY 10701

Stratton-Christian Press, Inc.
Box 1055
University Place Station
Des Moines, IA 50311

Superlearning, Inc.
450 Seventh Avenue, Suite 500
New York, NY 10123

Teachers and Writers Collaborative
84 Fifth Avenue
New York, NY 10011

The Booksource
6020 Ventura Canyon Avenue
Van Nuys, CA 90401

University of The Trees Press
P.O. Box 644
Boulder Creek, CA 95006

Zephyr Press
430 South Essex Lane
Tucson, AZ 85711

ABOUT THE AUTHOR

Karin Hess is presently the teacher/coordinator of an elementary school gifted program and an adjunct instructor at the college of New Rochelle, N.Y. where she earned a Master's Degree in Gifted Education. As national president of IMAGE (Institute for Maximizing Affective Growth in Education) she has travelled all over the United States to conduct seminars in imagery, creativity, writing and self-concept.

Ms. Hess has used the whole-person approach to teaching preschool through graduate school and has found that no matter what the age, it works! Imagery has been the most effective tool she's found to enhance the learning process.

Karin resides with her two sons and husband in a rural area of eastern Pennsylvania in their 150-year old farmhouse.